BREEDING A LITTER

A Complete Guide To Mating, Whelping And Puppy Rearing

J.M. Evans MRCVS

With Caroline Ackroyd Gibson

R

RINGPRESS

Published by Ringpress Books,
A Division of Interpet Publishing
Vincent Lane, Dorking, Surrey RH4 3YX

ISBN 10-1 86054 244 1
ISBN 13-978 1 86054 244 2

Printed and bound in Singapore

10 9 8 7 6 5 4 3 2 1

ACKNOWLEDGEMENTS

I freely admit that this book would not be in your hands were it not for the help, encouragement and expertise of a great supporting team. Producing the original manuscript, although time-consuming, is in fact just a small part of the process. I am grateful to all those at Interpet Publishing who have given advice in respect of content; they picked up many sins of omission and commission and, as a result, the book has matured considerably since its conception. Without their knowledge and skill, my aim, which was to produce a book that could be easily referred to at the time of need, would not have been met.

My special thanks go to Sue Bailey who typed the many drafts and final script against all odds. I am grateful also for the support and help given to me freely by a number of veterinary surgeons in practice and working in the veterinary pharmaceutical industry. My particular thanks go to Sarah Heath BVSc, MRCVS of the Association of Pet Behaviour Counsellors for her guidance concerning the latest developments in respect of modifying dog behaviour, and also to Susan Shaw BVSc, Msc, Dip ACVIM, MRCVS of Bristol University for her input into the section dealing with endo- and ectoparasites.

I acknowledge with gratitude the continuing support given to me by my wife, Monica. She has been an unfailing source of constructive criticism, and, as an author's spouse, she has put up with endless discussions and periods of distraction on my part, without complaint. This is truly the very last book (but one) I shall write, I promise – but I've said that before!

Finally, but by no means least, I must give credit to Caroline Ackroyd-Gibson, who was responsible for bringing me out of retirement. Her views as the experienced breeder of *Toraylac* Cavalier King Charles Spaniels were particularly helpful and pertinent when this book was in its formative stages. Her ideas and practical experience have helped, I think, to give balance to the text.

Finally, my aim in writing this book has been to try to make bringing puppies into this world – either by design or by accident – less traumatic and more satisfying. Hopefully, it will also lead to the production of healthy, well-balanced and well-mannered puppies, which will enable more owners to realise the many benefits and comfort that pet-owning can bring.

Jim Evans

CONTENTS

INTRODUCTION

I n writing this book our main aim is to help dog breeders produce sound, healthy puppies without any behavioural 'hang-ups', who fit snugly into today's society without causing embarrassment or friction.

More and more, it is being recognised that the prevention of inappropriate behaviour in dogs starts in the nest, since puppies are at the height of their learning ability between three and 12 weeks of age. Thus, it is particularly important for breeders to 'get it right', so that the puppies they raise have the best start in life. This should, in turn, help to ensure that their new owners can more realistically expect to achieve the goal of having an 'ideal dog', and to reap all the rewards that dog ownership can bring.

What we have to say will, we hope, be of use to all dog breeders, be they regular, occasional, unexpected, experienced or novice. We have concentrated on giving, in depth, all the background information that is needed to understand:
- What makes bitches 'tick'
- The mating process
- How to manage pregnant bitches
- What to do during whelping
- The intricacies of raising puppies
- The importance of preventive medicine
- How to shape a puppy's future behaviour.

We sincerely hope that everyone who reads this book will find something of interest and assistance, and be encouraged to help us achieve our aims. If that is indeed the case then our efforts will not have been in vain.

HOW TO USE THIS BOOK

By all means read this book from cover to cover – it should not take long and doubtless you will discover many facts that will be new to you. However, the book is principally designed to be used as a 'service manual'. The layout and cross-referencing we have adopted should allow any piece of information required to be readily and easily retrieved at the time of need.
- First, we have provided, very deliberately, a full contents list, which should be viewed as a first 'port of call' when data is sought.
- Secondly, a summary of the subjects covered is presented in a box at the beginning of each chapter.
- Thirdly, we have provided a glossary of the technical terms used.
- Finally, rather than write pages and pages of prose, we have summarised much of the data in tables and presented many lists of facts as so-called 'bullet points'.

Hopefully, you will find our efforts in this respect helpful.

Jim Evans

CHAPTER 1

TO BREED OR NOT TO BREED?

Currently, the dog population in the UK lies between five and six million and the estimated life span of dogs that survive past the first three months of their lives is calculated to be eight to ten years. Thus, since the dog population is relatively stable, approximately 600,000 replacement puppies must be born each year. But where do they come from, who breeds them and why?

The only reliable available statistic is that nearly 48,000 litters of pedigree puppies were registered with the Kennel Club in 2003. Of these the best estimate is that 9,000 litters were bred by regular breeders, i.e. those who produce two or more litters a year. The remainder, 39,000 litters, were produced by occasional breeders, i.e. those who own a pedigree bitch and just want one litter from their pet. Together, these breeders of pedigree dogs produce a little more than a 250,000 puppies; the average litter size is taken to be 5.5 pups. The remaining replacement puppies, just under 350,000, must come from owners of pedigree bitches who don't wish to register their litters, and from owners of mongrel or crossbreed bitches. It is frankly not known how many litters from these sources are the result of planned or unexpected pregnancies, but doubtless, a great number – especially those from mongrel bitches – must fall into the latter category.

No doubt many of the breeders in all the categories noted above (over

100,000), will find themselves in need of up-to-date, easily retrievable information relating to the whelping process, puppy rearing and other aspects of dog breeding. This book, which is deliberately set out like a manual, will hopefully meet this need.

In 1974 it was stated that nearly 900,000 puppies were destroyed as being surplus to requirements. According to recent RSPCA figures, in onr year that charity destroyed just 7,000 dogs and re-homed 22,000 dogs. Allowing for destructions by the other charities and by veterinary surgeons, the total number of dogs destroyed each year will be higher but probably by not more than five or ten fold, 35-70,000. This improvement on the 1974 figure has, no doubt, been brought about by the greatly increased number of spayed bitches in the dog population. There is, however, no room for complacency and Dogs Trust (previously called the NCDL) and other charities are right, in our view, to actively promote the spaying of pet bitches. We have therefore given detailed guidance on heat control in bitches and the prevention of unwanted pregnancies (see page 12).

On a similar note, it has been stated recently that more dogs are destroyed each year because of inappropriate behaviour (e.g. aggression, destructive behaviour and excessive barking) than die as a result of infectious disease. Like many dog behaviourists, we believe that this unfortunate situation could be limited if breeders paid particular attention to the habituation and socialisation of the puppies they raise, particularly from three weeks of age and onwards. This subject is dealt with throughout this book but especially in Chapter Eight.

BREEDER CATEGORIES
As noted in the introduction to this chapter, essentially breeders fall into three main categories:
- **Regular breeders:** owners of pedigree bitches who produce two or more litters a year.
- **Occasional breeders:** mainly the owners of pedigree bitches, but possibly the owners of mongrel or crossbreed bitches who wish to produce just a single litter or possibly two or three litters, no more frequently than one litter a year. Included in this group are the owners of bitches obtained on 'breeding terms'.
- **Unintentional breeders:** breeders whose bitches have been accidentally mated and where termination of the pregnancy was considered inappropriate, and those bitch owners faced with a totally unexpected pregnancy.

THE DECISION TO BREED

OBJECTIVES
It is important if you, as a bitch owner, are thinking of producing a litter to examine very closely *why* you should want to produce and rear a litter. Consider the questions noted below.

- As a pedigree bitch owner, are you really interested in your particular breed and feel that you would like to produce the ideal specimen for show purposes? If the answer is 'yes', you will undoubtedly need to become a regular breeder and must be prepared for all that entails. Are you willing and able to cover all the costs involved? These may include: constructing kennels, advertising litters, veterinary fees, payment for breeding stock and stud fees, feeding and other management costs. Don't go ahead unless you have the funds, the commitment and the time – this will be a full-time job!

- Are you considering producing a puppy from your own pedigree bitch for yourself, a relative or someone who just admires your pet? This is perfectly acceptable and quite common, but make sure that you can meet the costs associated with mating, whelping and raising a litter, and remember you need to find good homes for *all* the puppies. You are most unlikely to show much profit at the end of the day. Indeed, if your bitch needs a Caesarean section or other veterinary attention, you may well find yourself out of pocket. Money apart, it is most important that you ensure that you and your family have the real commitment that is needed. Don't underestimate the amount of time that raising a litter requires. Weigh up all the pros and cons carefully, and, if you are happy, 'go for it!'

- Are you tempted to breed simply to recoup some of the costs of obtaining your bitch and possibly make a profit, too? If that is the case then it is probably better to forget it. As noted above, very few people make much money from breeding the odd litter, and often it can turn out to be an expensive loss-making exercise. More often than not, the income from the sale of puppies does not cover the total expense involved in raising a litter – and that is without taking your time into consideration.

- Are you committed to have a litter through breeding terms? (This is a deal arranged with the breeder at the time of buying a bitch puppy.) If so, you have little choice but to go ahead. Do, however, check exactly what you are committed to do. In these circumstances, your aim should be to try to minimise the time involved, and any loss, by good management and making as sure as you can that the puppies will all be sold by six – or at the latest, eight – weeks of age.

- Are you thinking of having a litter for education purposes for your family? It is debatable how much children learn from such experiences, but you must judge that for yourself. However, do bear in mind the cost and time implications noted above, and the fact that your bitch could end up having her puppies in your vet's surgery and not at home where the whelping can be observed!

MEDICAL CONSIDERATIONS

Having decided to breed from your bitch, it is wise to ask your vet to check your bitch thoroughly to make sure that she has no serious physical, medical or inherited conditions or defects that would preclude breeding (see Chapter Seven). Quite apart from safety considerations for your bitch, it is quite unfair to puppy purchasers if you perpetuate some significant congenital flaw.

BEHAVIOURAL CONSIDERATIONS

Because many behavioural traits can be inherited, it is best to forget breeding from your bitch if her underlying character is in any way questionable. Do remember, however, that behaviour problems may be the result of a lack of, or inadequate, habituation and socialisation as a puppy and that aggression and destructiveness may have been caused by inappropriate training methods or the lack of a firm lead by the breeder of your bitch, or possibly a previous owner. If such underlying causes can be positively identified, and you are happy that the behaviour is acquired rather than inherited, then you could consider breeding. But it is important to be aware that if handling or other behaviour problems arise during mating or whelping, you could find yourself in difficulty.

PRACTICAL CONSIDERATIONS

- **Time:** For a day or two before the whelping is due, bitches need to be under reasonably close supervision. They should not be left alone for more than an hour or two without observation. Someone will have to attend the bitch during the whelping itself, which could last for as long as 24 hours or even more. Afterwards, the puppies will need to be kept clean and fed, and time must be allotted for interviewing prospective owners. In all, you should allow for at least four months of intensive care and attention to your bitch and her puppies, as it is not sensible to board her during pregnancy and nursing.
- **Health:** There is no evidence to support the popular view that having a litter is 'good' for bitches. However, apart from some possible hazards associated with giving birth and post-whelping, it is not likely

to be harmful either. Many of the small and some of the flat-faced breeds (e.g. Pekingese and Pugs) are more inclined to have whelping problems, thus extra thought is needed before breeding from them. A veterinary surgeon should be consulted if you have any doubts.

A great difference in the size of the two parents *could* result in the puppies being relatively oversized, which could mean a difficult whelping. If this is likely to be the case, it is wise to consult your veterinary surgeon early in the pregnancy. Having a crossbred or mongrel litter will not spoil or taint a bitch in any way, nor will it prevent her having a purebred litter later on.

- **Space:** An area will need to be set aside for the whelping. More importantly, the puppies will need space to run around in the home and garden for some weeks before they are ready to go to their new homes. During much of that time they will not be house-trained, and therefore an enclosed area in the home and a properly fenced area in the garden will be necessary.
- **Homing puppies:** Most puppies are ready to leave their mother by six to eight weeks old. It is more difficult to sell puppies during the summer holiday months or during mid-winter, so it is preferable to avoid producing a litter that will mature at these times.

Responsible bitch owners take care to ensure that the puppies they have raised only go to homes where they will be well looked after. It is easier to be sure about the homes of people you know, but otherwise lengthy discussions may be necessary to satisfy yourself that the puppies will be well cared for.

Unless you have very definite requests for puppies, it is wise to begin advertising locally when the puppies are three to four weeks old. Advertise in the local newspapers and put a card in the local newsagents' window. Some veterinary surgeons display 'homes wanted' cards in their waiting rooms. If your puppies are of an unusual or less saleable breed, advertisements in the dog press or national papers may be required.

Be suspicious of anyone who will not give reasonable particulars about themselves when enquiring about puppies for sale.

Finally, be prepared to have your puppies returned to you for re-homing should the original owners no longer be in a position to care for them. As a breeder this is your responsibility.

For a small fee, breeders of pedigree dogs can, when they register a litter with the Kennel Club, ask for the pups to be placed on the Club's Puppy Sales Register (PSR) to help sell the pups more promptly.

- **Insurance:** A number of insurance companies offer a variety of policies that give 'cover' for whelping bitches. Your veterinary surgeon will advise which is most suitable for your situation. Some policies will provide cover in respect of the puppies for a number of weeks after they have been sold. (See Chapter Six.)

HEAT CONTROL/CONTRACEPTION

If, after considering the points discussed above, you decide not to breed from your bitch, or if it is time for her to retire, you will want to consider preventing your bitch coming on heat. Apart from helping to reduce the number of unwanted puppies, this action offers many advantages for you and, more importantly, for your bitch.

The main reasons why bitch owners should control heat if they do not wish to breed at all, or when their bitch is 'retired', are:

• To gain a health advantage: The risk of the bitch developing uterine problems (particularly pyometra) and suffering from false pregnancy or vaginal hyperplasia is eliminated, and the incidence of mammary tumours is much reduced (see Chapter Two: Feminine problems).

• To prevent unwanted pregnancy.

• To make the female pet more consistently companionable: A bitch's temperament changes during heat and metoestrus, especially if she suffers from false pregnancy.

• To make owning a bitch more convenient: To avoid problems of messy bleeding, unsightly vulval swelling, attractiveness to dogs and the need to keep the bitch confined for two to three weeks twice a year.

• To reduce any tendency to wander with the possibility of being run over, lost or causing a road traffic accident.

Bitches are generally neutered *after* their first heat, but new bitch owners should discuss the subject with their vet before the bitch's first season.

Heat control can be achieved by spaying, complete surgical removal of the uterus and ovaries under general anaesthetic, or by chemical methods. Surgery is the most common procedure and offers the advantage of permanence. However, some bitches – particularly in the large breeds – do not spay well, and may suffer from urinary incontinence subsequently. In other bitches, anaesthesia may be considered too risky. In these cases – or where temporary heat control is required – a chemical method involving the administration of an artificial hormone similar to that used in the human 'pill', may be advocated. Be prepared to discuss the pros and cons associated with each method (see Table 1) with your vet.

Pregnancy can be terminated if a bitch has been seen to be accidentally mated (see page 28), but prevention is much the better option.

TABLE 1: SPAYING – THE FACTS

Timing
Some vets advocate spaying before the first heat, but it is generally better to let the bitch experience the hormonal changes associated with at least one heat before surgery so that she becomes fully mature, both physically and mentally. The operation should not be carried out when the bitch is on heat, nor during the two-month period after a bitch has been on heat, and certainly not if she is showing signs of false pregnancy.

Pros
- To gain a health advantage: It is good preventive medicine.
- To prevent an unwanted pregnancy and the production of unwanted puppies.
- Bitch owning is made more convenient: less mess, no persistent male interest.
- Bitches are more consistently companionable and are less inclined to wander.
- Provides peace of mind for the owner.
- The operation provides permanent heat control – any costs are 'one off'.
- Spaying is effective and generally quite safe.

Cons
- A major surgical operation, which may possibly carry an anaesthetic risk and post-operative problems, such as wound infection. The risks are higher when the operation is carried out on overweight, elderly bitches.
- Some bitches, particularly in the large breeds, may develop a degree of urinary incontinence,
- In some breeds a coat change may be seen after the operation. Spaniels, Retrievers and Collies may develop a more woolly coat, and short-haired breeds (e.g. Dobermanns) may develop bald patches on their flanks.
- The operation is irreversible.
- Some spayed bitches put on weight after the operation. This can usually be prevented by dietary control and proper exercise. Regularly weighing spayed bitches is a sensible precaution.
- May be considered costly, but, in the long-term, spaying is cost-effective. For senior citizens and people on income support, charities such as Dogs Trust (formerly the NCDL) offer spaying at a substantially reduced cost.

CHAPTER 2

THE SEXUAL CYCLE

In this chapter, we give up-to-date background scientific information relating to the sexual (oestrous) cycle in bitches. We hope that this will be of interest and help to all breeders, including those who produce litters regularly, and lead to a better understanding of the mating process, pregnancy and whelping.

First, we describe the external signs shown by bitches during their oestrous cycle. Secondly, we examine the anatomy of the bitch's reproductive organs; thirdly, we detail the background physiological changes that make bitches 'tick'. An understanding of these matters will help owners to:

- Keep their bitch healthy
- Identify early any conditions that need veterinary attention
- Facilitate successful breeding
- Lead to the production of sound, fit puppies
- Communicate with vets, veterinary nurses and breeders more effectively, and lead to a better understanding of the advice given
- Make bitch owning more fulfilling and rewarding.

HEAT IN BITCHES

ONSET

The onset of puberty is marked by bitches 'coming on heat' or being 'in season'. The majority of bitches reach this stage when they are about six to seven months old, but in some it can be as early as four months or even as late as two years of age.

Bitches who follow the normal sequence of events usually breed more successfully. If you want a litter from your bitch, ask a vet to check her if she has not come in season by the time she is 18 months old.

SIGNS

In most bitches, heat occurs in two stages, *pro oestrus* and *oestrus*, each lasting about nine days. However, the duration of heat in total, and of each stage, can be very variable between individual animals as well as between different heats in the same bitch. (See figure 1.)

During *pro oestrus* the bitch's vulva is swollen and there is a blood-stained discharge. Although the bitch will be attractive to dogs, she does not usually allow them to mate at this time.

In the second stage (*oestrus*) the vulva becomes further enlarged and turgid, and the discharge becomes straw-coloured rather than blood-stained. Characteristically, by definition, bitches will accept the male during this stage of heat.

Ovulation – the liberation of eggs from the ovaries – occurs spontaneously about two days after the onset of the second stage (*oestrus*), i.e. about 11 days after the first signs of heat are seen.

SUBSEQUENT EVENTS

In unmated bitches, heat is followed by a period, known as *metoestrus*, which lasts for about 90 days (technically, divided into two phases – see Fig. 1.) The beginning and end of this stage is not usually marked by any obvious external signs, but, as a result of the hormonal changes taking place, many bitches show signs of false pregnancy at this time.

Metoestrus is followed by a period of sexual inactivity, known as *an-oestrus*, which lasts on average two-and-a-half months, but its duration can be extremely variable.

FREQUENCY

It is principally the variation in the length of the final stage, *an-oestrus*, which determines the frequency of heat in bitches. The normal interval between heats is five to 10 months; intervals of less than four months

FIGURE 1: THE OESTROUS CYCLE OF THE BITCH

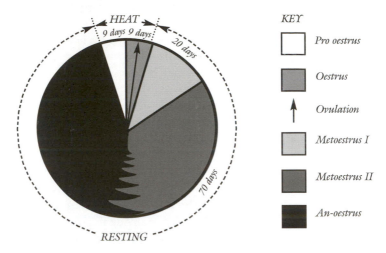

may be associated with infertility. However, breed variability can be striking; for example, German Shepherds commonly come on heat as frequently as every four to four-and-a-half months, whereas African breeds, such as the Basenji, tend to be in season only once a year. Pregnancy increases the interval to the next heat by about one month.

ANATOMY

THE OVARIES
Like other female mammals, bitches have two ovaries; they are situated just behind each kidney. At birth, bitch puppies have close to one million eggs in their ovaries. These decline in number to about 350,000 at maturity, and to a tenth of that number by the time they are five years of age. Under the influence of hormones (chemical messengers), cells in the ovaries group together to form follicles, which are fluid-filled cyst-like structures. Some of the inner cells in the follicles develop into eggs. The follicles containing eggs work their way to the surface of the ovary; they rupture to release eggs and then collapse to form solid bodies called corpora lutea (singular corpus luteum). The ovaries of adult bitches contain all these developmental stages.

THE OVIDUCTS
These are two thin tubes, which convey eggs from the ovaries into the

uterine horns. The ends of the oviducts, which lie against the ovaries, are funnel-shaped and fringed to facilitate the capture of eggs.

THE UTERUS (WOMB)

This is a hollow muscular organ with a short body and two long horns. The horns are narrow in non-pregnant bitches, but during pregnancy they dilate considerably to contain the developing puppies.

The cervix is located at the lower (posterior) end of the uterus. This protrudes into the vagina. The cervix is normally closed, but it opens when a bitch is 'on heat' (to allow the passage of sperm into the uterus) and again at whelping (to allow the puppies to be born).

FIGURE 2: THE FEMALE GENITAL TRACT

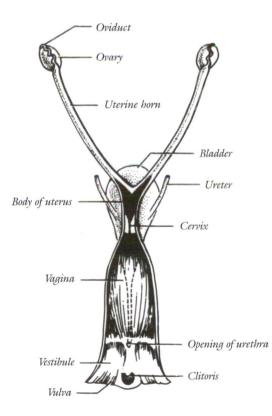

THE VAGINA
Bitches have a very long vagina. This organ is hollow, muscular and capable of considerable dilation.

THE VULVA
This is the external opening of the bitch's genital tract, which becomes much enlarged when the bitch is 'on heat'.

THE MAMMARY GLANDS
The mammary glands of the bitch are paired and are situated in rows down either side of the chest and abdominal wall. Usually there are 10 glands in number; sometimes one or two pairs of glands may be missing.

FIGURE 3: THE SITUATION OF THE MAMMARY GLANDS

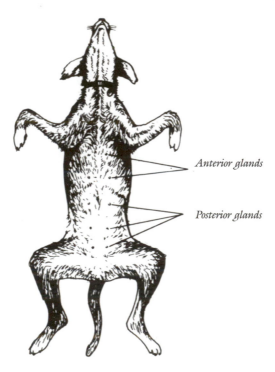

Anterior glands

Posterior glands

PHYSIOLOGY

This rather scientific section is included for those breeders who are particularly interested in knowing exactly what makes bitches tick, or who feel they need the detail to better understand the mating process, pregnancy, whelping, and the various diseases and conditions that affect bitches. An understanding of these technicalities is not particularly important or necessary for occasional breeders.

Technically, bitches are termed mon-oestrus; they ovulate (shed eggs) only once each breeding season.

HORMONES

Three groups of hormones are involved in bringing about the oestrous cycle in bitches:

❶ The releasing factors come from an area of the brain called the hypothalamus. They control the production and release of the gonadotrophins.

❷ The gonadotrophins, three in number, are produced by the anterior pituitary gland in the brain.
- **Follicle Stimulating Hormone (FSH):** stimulates eggs to grow in the ovaries
- **Luteinizing Hormone (LH):** stimulates the release of eggs from the follicles
- **Luteotrophic factors (prolactin):** promote the formation of, and maintain, the life of the corpora lutea in the ovaries and also stimulate the mammary glands to produce milk.

❸ The sex hormones oestrogen and progesterone.
- **Oestrogen:** produced by the eggs in the ovaries, it is responsible for producing the outward signs of heat (vulval swelling, bleeding and attractiveness to dogs) and for preparing the genital organs for reproduction including coitus (see also Table 2).
- **Progesterone:** produced by corpora lutea in the ovaries, this hormone is essential for the maintenance of pregnancy (see also Table 2).

Two other hormones play an important role during parturition (whelping):
- **Oxytocin:** This hormone is produced by the posterior pituitary gland in the brain, and causes the muscle cells in the wall of the uterus to contract. It plays a major role in the expulsion of the young at birth. The hormone also plays a part in the 'let down' of milk.
- **Relaxin:** This hormone is produced by the placenta soon after the

fertilised eggs are implanted. The hormone is not detected in non-pregnant bitches, including those that are showing signs of false pregnancy. Relaxin is responsible for bringing about relaxation of the muscles in the wall of the uterus, and induces relaxation of the pelvis before whelping. Its presence in the bloodstream can be used to confirm pregnancy.

Note: All these hormones are used therapeutically by a veterinary surgeon for a number of purposes, for example, in cases of infertility, to maintain pregnancy, in contraception, to assist the whelping process, and to empty the uterus after whelping.

PHEROMONES

This is the name given to a group of chemicals produced by the external surfaces of the body, which are used in communication between animals of the same species. Classically, a pheromone produced by a bitch's vagina when on heat attracts male dogs and stimulates sexual arousal. Synthetic pheromones, which mimic the effect of a pheromone produced by the skin around the mammary glands in lactating bitches, have been developed recently and are used to calm anxious and nervous dogs, for example those that have an accentuated fear (phobia) of fireworks.

HORMONAL INTERACTION

In the female there is an inborn cyclical activity in the hypothalamus, which is in fundamental control of reproductive function. However, this part of the brain is sensitive to both environmental factors and internal stimulae from the genital tract. The oestrous cycle is, therefore, controlled by a complex interplay between the hypothalamus and the reproductive tract, with the anterior pituitary acting as a central relay.

Figure 4 summarises the effects of the hormones produced by the anterior pituitary (the gonadotrophins), which are controlled by the releasing factors secreted from the hypothalamus; and those secreted by the ovaries (the sex hormones).

Follicle stimulating hormone (FSH) is secreted by the anterior pituitary gland in the brain and controls the development of the ovarian follicles, which in turn secrete oestrogen. At low levels this sex hormone exerts a positive feedback, stimulating more FSH to be released, resulting in further follicular growth and increased oestrogen levels. This process continues until the follicles are mature and about to rupture. At

FIGURE 4: THE INTERACTION BETWEEN THE
GONADOTROPHINS AND THE SEX HORMONES

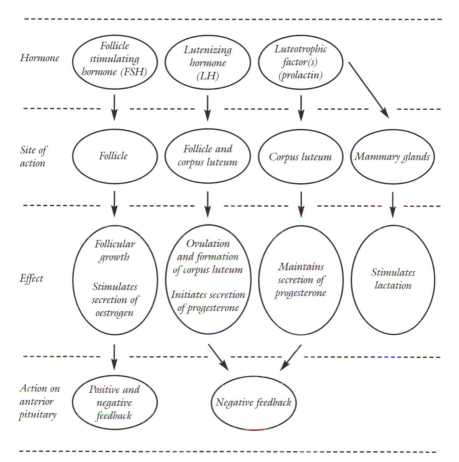

this stage the higher levels of oestrogen have a negative feedback effect, inhibiting FSH secretion, and probably triggering the release of luteinizing hormone (LH) from the anterior pituitary in a pulse, which causes ovulation.

The ruptured follicle is rapidly converted into a solid glandular body, the corpus luteum. The development of the corpora lutea is initiated in response to LH, and is maintained by the luteotrophic factor(s) (prolactin). The corpora lutea secrete progesterone, which has a negative feedback effect at high concentrations, inhibiting the secretion of the gonadotrophin, which maintain these secretory bodies. In essence, it is the balance of the two sex hormones – oestrogen and progesterone – that ultimately control the oestrous cycle by their feedback mechanisms. They also bring about changes in the accessory sex organs as illustrated in Table 2.

TABLE 2: THE EFFECTS OF THE SEX HORMONES ON THE GENITAL TRACT AND MAMMARY GLANDS

Sex hormones	Target accessory sex organ	Effect
Oestrogen	Lining of the uterus (the endometrium)	Proliferation of glands
	The muscular wall of the uterus (the myometrium)	Relaxation
	The cervix	Relaxation
	The vagina	Proliferation of the cells lining the vagina
	The mammary glands	Duct proliferation
Progesterone	Endometrium	Stimulates the glands in the lining of the uterus to produce mucus and other fluids
	Mammary glands	Growth of the milk-producing cells

HORMONE LEVELS

The hormonal profile during the oestrous cycle of the bitch is illustrated in figures 5, 6 and 7 (pages 23-24). The bitch is unusual in a number of ways:

❶ Low progesterone levels are present before ovulation.
❷ Standing oestrus, acceptance of the male, occurs as oestrogen levels fall and progesterone levels in the blood begin to rise.
❸ There is a long period of progesterone dominance in the non-pregnant, as well as the pregnant, bitch.

22

FIGURE 5: OESTROGEN, PROGESTERONE AND LH BLOOD LEVELS DURING PRO OESTRUS AND OESTRUS

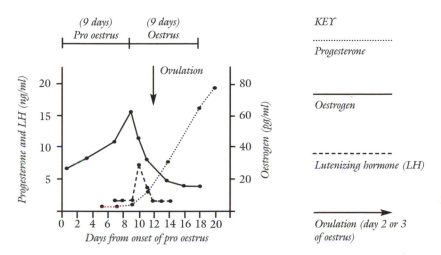

FIGURE 6: COMPARATIVE HORMONE LEVELS IN PREGNANT AND UNMATED/NON-PREGNANT BITCHES (ADAPTED FROM JÖCHLE, 1987)

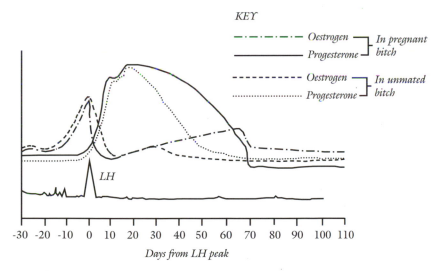

The levels of progesterone and oestrogen are virtually identical at the time when pregnancy diagnosis is needed (i.e. usually 20-30 days after ovulation), whether or not the bitch is pregnant. This means that measuring levels of these hormones is not relevant in respect of pregnancy diagnosis.

FIGURE 7: PROLACTIN LEVELS IN PREGNANT AND NON-PREGNANT BITCHES (ADAPTED FROM JÖCHLE, 1987)

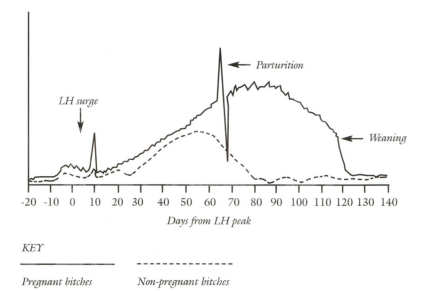

Days from LH peak

KEY

Pregnant bitches	*Non-pregnant bitches*

FEMININE PROBLEMS (RELATING TO THE OESTROUS CYCLE)

FALSE PREGNANCY

This is the condition in which bitches show the signs of pregnancy, nursing and lactation, and yet produce no puppies – either because they have not been mated or have failed to conceive.

The signs of false pregnancy occur one to two months after the bitch has been on heat, and vary greatly in type and severity. Most bitches will produce some milk and display maternal behaviour. Many will have nervous signs, including restlessness, carrying shoes and toys around the house and taking them to their beds. A bitch that has suffered from the condition once is likely to experience it again after each subsequent heat, with the signs becoming progressively more severe and protracted.

Essentially, the condition can be regarded as normal, as about 60 per cent of bitches have false pregnancies to some degree. False pregnant bitches are capable of nursing a litter from a bitch that has died, so originally in the wild, and now in breeding kennels, the condition can serve a useful purpose.

If the signs are mild, it is probably better not to give any medication or treatment. The nervous signs will disappear more quickly if the bitch is denied sympathy, and if toys and brooding objects are removed. Less milk will be produced if exercise levels are increased and the carbohydrate content of the diet reduced. It can help to limit the bitch's water intake, but access to water must certainly not be prevented entirely.

If the signs are severe and the above actions do not help, veterinary advice should be sought. Hormone tablets or injections may help to relieve the signs, and, in some cases, bathing the mammary glands may be advised to help the milk dry up. Sedatives may be required to control the nervous signs. Owners are often advised to have their bitch spayed if she has severe false pregnancies, since bitches that do not come on heat do not suffer from false pregnancy. The chemical control of heat, with regular hormone injections, may also help to reduce the incidence of the condition and may be advocated by vets in some instances.

PYOMETRA

In this condition, large amounts of fluid accumulate in the uterus, characteristically one to two months after a bitch has been on heat. The cause is not entirely clear, but is probably brought about by an hormonal imbalance.

Typically, bitches with pyometra are obviously ill and depressed; they drink large amounts of water and urinate more frequently. The abdomen is often distended, and the bitch may have a raised temperature. In so-called 'open' cases there is a thick reddish-brown evil-smelling discharge from the vulva; there is no discharge in 'closed' cases. The condition is more often seen in older bitches, six to seven years of age, that have not had puppies, but that is by no means always the case. The condition has been reported in some bitches after their first heat, but this is extremely rare. The signs can be variable, so that diagnosis is not always easy.

If an owner suspects that their bitch is suffering from this condition, it is essential that veterinary advice is sought without delay since an emergency operation to remove the uterus and ovaries is usually needed to save the bitch. Some open cases may respond to medical treatment, and this course of action may be advised in animals in which anaesthesia and major surgery may be considered more risky.

MAMMARY TUMOURS

As many as 75 per cent of bitches develop mammary tumours (growths in the mammary glands) as they get older. It therefore makes sense to inspect the mammary glands of bitches regularly so that any swellings can be identified early. This is done preferably when the bitch is on heat and then again about a month later.

If lumps are felt, their size should be recorded and monitored carefully under veterinary supervision. Advice should be taken on their possible removal before the tumour has a chance to spread to other organs in the body – a situation that occurs all too often. Fortunately, many such growths are not malignant and are relatively easily removed, provided they have not been allowed to grow too large. It may be sufficient to excise just the growth itself, but sometimes one or more of the mammary glands and the associated lymph nodes may also need to be removed surgically.

TABLE 3: OTHER DISEASES AND CONDITIONS AFFECTING BITCHES

Condition/disease	Cause	Treatment/prevention
ABORTION Giving birth early or resorption of the young in the womb at an early stage in their development.	• Infection, either bacterial (ß haemolytic streptococci), viral (canine herpes virus), or toxoplasma. • Persistent high temperature. • Hormone imbalance. • Poor nutrition. • Trauma. • Teratogenic agents.	Seek veterinary help since effective treatment depends on an accurate diagnosis of the cause. Practise good husbandry and management of pregnant bitches, and avoid stress and over exercise. Don't give medicines during pregnancy without veterinary advice. Don't breed again from affected bitches.
NYMPHOMANIA Increased sexual activity (libido). Possibly more frequent heats.	Unclear but may be due to larger or more persistent follicles in the ovaries.	Seek veterinary help. Controlled by spaying the bitch or the use of chemicals to control heat.
AGALACTIA Failure to produce milk.	See Chapter 6.	See Chapter 6.
CYSTITIS Inflammation of the urinary bladder, leading to the	Usually a bacterial infection coming from the genital organs. May be	Veterinary assistance is required to obtain the most appropriate antibiotic. Surgical

frequent passing of urine or attempts to pass urine.	associated with stones in the bladder.	treatment may be required. Access to a plentiful water supply and avoiding situations where bitches may refrain from urinating for long periods may help to prevent the condition.
ECLAMPSIA Convulsive seizures after whelping.	See Chapter 6.	See Chapter 6.
INFERTILITY Failure to produce young.	See Chapter 3.	See Chapter 3.
MASTITIS Inflammation of the mammary glands.	See Chapter 6.	See Chapter 6.
METRITIS Inflammation of the uterus.	See Chapter 6.	See Chapter 6.
VAGINAL HYPERPLASIA Swelling of the lining of the vagina, which may protrude through the vulva. This condition is seen more commonly in Boxers and in Bulldogs.	Hormonal imbalances.	Veterinary treatment required, including possibly the administration of antibiotics, hormones or the surgical removal of the swelling.
VAGINAL POLYPS Smooth-rounded growths on the lining of the vagina.	Hormonal imbalances.	Surgical removal by a veterinary surgeon is required if the polyps are large or causing problems.
VAGINITIS Inflammation of the vagina.	Usually a bacterial infection but may be associated with trauma.	Prompt veterinary treatment, usually involving the administration of antibiotics, is required.

MISMATING/MISALLIANCE

If it is known that a bitch has been accidentally mated, veterinary help should be sought without delay. Action needs to be taken promptly, as an oestrogen injection or the start of a course of injections must be given within three to seven days of the mating, to avert pregnancy. These injections, which are unfortunately not always effective and may be associated with adverse side effects, will often cause the bitch to begin her heat all over again – and she may be even more willing to be mated on the second occasion. Adequate control measures to ensure that the bitch is not mated again will be particularly important in that situation.

Quite recently a product containing a compound that acts as a progesterone antagonist has been introduced. Two injections are needed 24 hours apart and they can be given much later in pregnancy – from 0-45 days after mating. However, early administration is more effective. Your veterinary surgeon will advise what course of action is most appropriate in any particular case. The options will be greater if you seek help early.

In cases of suspected mismating/misalliance, owners should be prepared to provide their veterinary surgeon with a full history of the occurrence. Sometimes swabs are taken from the vagina to establish whether or not a mating has taken place.

It is dangerous to the bitch's health to rely continually on averting pregnancy after mismating; adequate *preventive* measures must be considered. In the case of bitches not intended for breeding, spaying is generally the action of choice. Vets will sometimes advise that bitches are spayed three to four weeks after the mismating rather than giving misalliance hormone injections and then spaying the bitch later.

UNEXPECTED PREGNANCY

In the case of bitches who are unexpectedly found to be pregnant, spaying, removing the uterus with the foetuses inside at the same time, is often the action of choice. If this is not practical, or if the bitch is wanted for breeding in the future, the only option is to allow the pregnancy to proceed and for whelping to take place naturally.

CHAPTER 3

MATING

Responsible breeders ensure that the mating pair have not only been carefully selected, but that they have also been carefully prepared for the mating. In the bitch's case, it is vital to ensure that she is in optimum health for pregnancy, whelping and rearing her litter, which includes factors such as age, diet, and her general level of health.

AGE CONSIDERATIONS

It is best for a bitch to have her first litter between the ages of 16 months and two-and-a-half years, depending on the breed, and preferably not after five years of age if being bred for the first time. Most bitches begin their breeding career at about their third heat. For registered breeders, the Kennel Club has rules governing when bitches should have their first litter and the number of subsequent litters and their spacing.

If you are thinking about having further litters, you will need to take into consideration the following factors:
• The size of the previous litter
• The condition of your bitch after rearing the previous litter

- The anticipated cycle interval
- The ease of whelping
- The bitch's age in comparison to the norm for the breed
- The mothering behaviour of the bitch.

Be prepared to make the decision that having another litter is not the best thing for your bitch.

CHOOSING A SIRE

There is a considerable advantage to be gained by going to a *proven* stud dog, who is kept for the purpose and is known to sire strong puppies of good temperament and free from hereditary problems. In those breeds where it is relevant, check that the stud dog has undergone the necessary examinations to show that he is clear of hereditary problems, such as hip dysplasia (malformation of the hip joint) or eye disease (e.g. progressive retinal atrophy). See also Chapter Seven. It makes sense, of course, to visit the dog to satisfy yourself that he is of the type you like, and that he is of good temperament. There is a good deal of variation even within breeds!

The mating arrangements are best left in the hands of an experienced stud dog owner, who will handle any problems that might occur. Ask the stud dog owner for a view about the compatibility of the dog and bitch's pedigrees – will they 'click'? Line-breeding is acceptable, but too close in-breeding can result in the perpetuation of inherited anatomical and behavioural faults.

If you do arrange the mating yourself, try to make sure that the sire is experienced if the bitch is not, and vice versa. If you are a novice, it could be a big mistake to settle for the pet dog of a friend, since you will miss out on the expertise of an established breeder and their contacts, which incidentally can be a great help when it comes to selling the puppies.

In short, it is sensible to contact the breeder of your bitch and ask for help in finding a suitable stud. The experience of a knowledgeable breeder and stud dog handler is a most useful asset, especially if problems are encountered. Failing that, join a local canine society or breed club where you will find plenty of people willing to give you advice – and don't forget that your veterinary surgeon is also a good source of valuable guidance and helpful contacts.

When choosing a stud, it is wise to remember that you may need to take your bitch to be mated on the particular day *she* decides, and then possibly again two days later. Make sure there is no impediment to you being able to do this at short notice, whatever the weather!

Finally, be aware that even after carefully selecting a dog and arranging the mating, either the dog or the bitch may refuse to get together. In this case, it is wiser to abandon the arrangements with that dog. It always makes sense to have a reserve stud dog arranged, as it can be difficult to find a suitable dog at short notice.

As a separate issue, owners of stud dogs should note that it is sensible to disinfect the dogs penis and sheath soon after mating. Ask a veterinary surgeon to recommend the most suitable product. Some regular antiseptics may not be appropriate or safe.

PEDIGREES

A pedigree dog is one whose sire, dam and breeding line have been certified by the breeder. Although not compulsory, all thoroughbred pedigree breeding stock should be registered with the Kennel Club. The owner can then sell puppies as pedigree stock (see Appendix 2). In order to complete the Kennel Club's Puppy Registration form, you will need the details relating to the stud dog and his owner's name, address and signature. Don't forget to obtain this at the time of a successful mating.

MONGRELS

The great majority of mongrel puppies (those where neither the sire nor dam is purebred) are, no doubt, produced as the result of an unplanned pregnancy, so the selection of a sire is largely irrelevant. However, if you have a mongrel bitch and would like to mate her to a specific dog, do ensure that the dog is of similar size to your bitch, that he is healthy, has no obvious deformities and, importantly, that he is of good temperament. Subsequently, follow the advice given above and under the headings 'Mating' and 'The mating process – step by step' later in this chapter. Do take care not to get bitten or allow the dog to hurt your bitch.

FEEDING POTENTIAL BREEDING STOCK

BITCHES

Before mating, breeding bitches should be fed the correct quantity of a prepared balanced diet to ensure that they are in good, hard condition, and the right weight for their size and breed. Supplementation of a breeding bitch's diet with vitamins and minerals should not be required if a commercially produced complete balanced food is given in accordance with the company's recommendation. Including such additives in excess can be counterproductive, and may possibly even lead to adverse effects.

STUD DOGS

All that is really necessary to note in respect of feeding stud dogs is that they should be given a good, balanced diet containing sufficient protein, fat, carbohydrate, fibre, minerals and vitamins. This requirement can be met most satisfactorily by feeding a complete prepared food from a reputable manufacturer.

Note: For occasional breeders, it is a matter of personal choice whether a dry or wet diet is used. However, particularly in a kennel situation, dry food does have a number of advantages and is probably the product of choice for regular breeders. This is because: it is less messy, it is easier to measure the correct amount for each dog, storage is simpler, and the food can be left down for longer without attracting flies and other insects.

HEALTH CARE BEFORE MATING

Needless to say, you should only consider breeding from a bitch that is fit and in generally good condition. She should be lean and hard as a result of feeding a complete, nutritious diet and from being given appropriate and regular exercise.

Before your bitch is mated, it is advisable to take her to your veterinary surgeon for a thorough health check. Be prepared for him to refer you to a specialist, who will carry out examinations and possibly tests to make sure that your bitch is not suffering from any inherited problems, such as: hip dysplasia, heart disease, eye conditions, patella dislocation etc. The tests carried out will vary according to the breed, and it may be necessary to see more than one specialist consultant – your vet will advise. (See Chapter Seven: Inherited Diseases and Conditions.)

This is also the time to ask your vet about the possible need for booster vaccinations, worming and the eradication or prevention of ecto-parasite infestations (see Chapter Seven).

It is also relevant to note that some stud dog owners request that a vaginal swab from the bitch is examined bacteriologically before she is mated. Your vet will undertake this for you and will advise whether any medication, such as the administration of an antibiotic injection or a course of antibiotic tablets, is required. Similarly, it can make sense for bitch owners to ask that preputial swabs taken from the stud dog are examined bacteriologically before mating to help minimise the risk of the bitch becoming infected. This action is of particular importance in the case of regular breeders, who have a number of breeding bitches, to help prevent the introduction of an infection into the kennel.

MATING

Mating in bitches has been described in depth by a number of authors. The details noted below represent, in summary, a consensus view.

BEHAVIOUR

As noted earlier, bitches are attractive to males for about nine days while they are in the first stage of heat, *pro oestrus*. At this time, attempts at mounting by the male are usually actively rejected. Mating will be allowed when the bitch is in 'standing heat', that is about two days after the onset of *oestrus*, or about 11 days after heat was first noted. Before mounting a bitch, the male may go through a relatively prolonged courtship procedure, but, more generally, the male will simply briefly lick the bitch's vulva before mounting – that is certainly the case with experienced stud dogs.

As a result of this attention, the bitch will usually stand firmly with her tail held to one side, exposing the vulva. Because the dog has a small bone in his penis, penetration is achieved without erection. Once inside the vagina, the glandular part of the penis becomes engorged with blood and this is accompanied by strong thrusting movements, resulting in the ejaculation of the first part of the semen, which consists mainly of fluid from the prostate gland.

Once pelvic thrusting ends, the male will dismount, with his penis still within the bitch's vagina. By turning and lifting one hind leg over the bitch, the dog will end up 'tied' to her, tail to tail (see Figure 8), locked by the engorged penis which, together with the contractions of the vaginal muscles after coitus, makes separation difficult. During the 'tie', ejaculation of seminal fluid continues; this second part is rich in spermatozoa (see Figure 8). No attempt should be made to separate animals locked in this way since the dog will be released in good time. Buckets of cold water thrown over the animals simply wet them and do little or nothing to speed up the separation process.

The events described above are the norm and what most breeders expect from an experienced stud dog. However, it should be noted that the 'tie' is *not* essential for conception; many bitches become pregnant after only the briefest of encounters.

The tie can last anything from five minutes to one hour (average 20 minutes), and during this time the bitch and the dog may drag each other around. Although possibly disconcerting to the novice breeder,

FIGURE 8: MATING – COITAL POSITIONS

Mounting

The 'tie'

this behaviour is not usually a cause for concern and seldom results in damage to either animal. However, it is sensible to remain on hand and to be prepared to restrain the dog and the bitch if the movement is excessive. The tie finally breaks quite spontaneously, and some of the seminal fluid will be seen draining from the bitch's vulva. This is no cause for concern because it consists principally of the mostly sperm-free third fraction of the ejaculate and there is no need to follow the ancient ritual of holding the bitch up by her hind legs!

TIMING OF MATING

Traditionally, bitches are mated twice, 11 and 13 days after the onset of *pro oestrus*, to help ensure that spermatozoa are present in the female tract at, or around, the time of ovulation. This 'rule of thumb' method, observation of vulval turgidity and the presence of a straw-coloured discharge, and encouraging behavioural signs from the bitch is generally very successful. Canine sperm have unusual longevity and can remain viable in the female genital tract – and capable of fertilising eggs – for as long as a week.

Much time can be lost if matings are ineffectual, because bitches ovulate on average only every six months. There is thus an urgent need to 'get it right' on each occasion. This has led to the development and employment of more scientific techniques, which are particularly relevant when a visit to the stud dog of choice necessitates a protracted and expensive journey. Doubtless many fertility problems result from arranging a mating to take place at a *convenient* time, when travel is easier, rather than on the most *appropriate* day.

If the time when eggs are released from the ovaries can be more precisely determined than is possible by simply observing the external signs and behaviour shown by bitches, fertility rates are likely to be increased. Furthermore, the expected whelping date can be predicted more precisely, conception failures are less likely, and the management of the bitch can be simplified (see below).

DETECTION OF OVULATION

Three more precise methods of detecting ovulation are available to veterinary surgeons in practice: vaginal cytology (the microscopic examination of smears taken from the vagina to quantify the different cell types present), vaginoscopy (detecting changes in the lining of the vagina using a special instrument), and the measurement of hormone levels in the bitch's blood (either by the vet himself or with the aid of a specialist veterinary laboratory).

Technological advances in the measurement of hormone levels have resulted in a simple, quick method of measuring levels of progesterone, the hormone responsible for maintaining pregnancy, in just a small blood sample taken from the bitch. Progesterone levels start to rise just before ovulation (see Chapter Two). The results can be obtained within half an hour of taking the sample. This enables veterinary surgeons to advise bitch owners whether ovulation is about to occur, or has just occurred, so that mating can be timed to take place during the period of peak fertility.

For bitches who have been previously bred from successfully, a single sample taken 10 to 11 days after the onset of heat will normally suffice. Owners will need, however, to be prepared to have the bitch mated within two days. In the case of bitches who have failed to get in whelp previously, more frequent sampling may be needed, but it is unlikely that there will be a need to test more than three samples.

In short, the availability of a simple method of measuring progesterone levels in the blood can potentially save breeders unnecessary costs, help to ensure a successful mating, maximise litter size and minimise the number of disappointed potential puppy owners. Furthermore, it will help vets to determine the likely whelping date and thus decide more reliably when to carry out a Caesarean operation if that becomes necessary.

More recently, an instrument developed in Poland, which measures the changing electrical resistance in vaginal mucus at, and around, the time of ovulation, has been made available to veterinary surgeons, veterinary nurses and regular breeders. For further information, visit www.draminski.com

When planning to mate your bitch, it is wise to discuss with your veterinary surgeon whether it is sensible to apply any of these tests in your particular case.

MATING: STEP BY STEP

STEP 1
- Observe your bitch closely, starting two or three weeks before she is due in season. Your records should tell you when this should be expected. Look for the signs noted below, which generally indicate that a bitch is about to come 'on heat':
    - More frequent urination
    - Some inappetance (reluctance to eat)
    - Abdominal pain
    - Spots of blood from the vulva – *start counting the days*
    - More frequent licking of the vulva
    - Vulval swelling
    - Interest by male dogs.
- Bitches vary considerably, and not every bitch will show all the signs listed.

STEP 2
- Once the vulval discharge changes from blood-stained to straw-coloured and the vulva becomes more swollen and turgid, anticipate that ovulation will occur in about two days. This is usually about 11 days after blood spotting was first seen. However, as noted earlier, the timing of ovulation can be very variable between bitches and even at

different heats in the same bitch. The situation is further complicated by the fact that a few bitches will fail to show the normal signs of heat (so-called silent heat) and yet still conceive.

- Make arrangements to have your bitch mated, preferably twice, on days 11 and 13, but be guided somewhat by the stud dog himself. You will need to fit in with the bitch rather than vice versa, so be prepared to travel at short notice. Feed your bitch the night before but not on the day of mating itself.
- In the case of bitches who have failed to conceive previously, or who are showing any abnormalities of the oestrous cycle, consult your vet about the advisability of carrying out one of the tests described earlier to detect the time of ovulation.

STEP 3
- Allow your bitch and the stud dog to interact on their own for a short while, but keep your bitch on the lead if there are any signs of aggression.
- Once the dog shows interest, hold your bitch from in front to allow the dog to mount.
- Keep hold of your bitch while the dog is thrusting.
- Once thrusting stops, the dog will usually dismount on his own, but if this action does not occur, lift one of the dog's hind legs over the bitch so that they are tied together back to back, and hold one or both of them still until they separate naturally. You will probably need to wait for 30 minutes or so, but it can be an hour or even more! (See Figure 8, page 34.)
- Leave your bitch to her own devices once separated, but offer her a drink and maybe a tidbit of food.
- After a successful mating, the owner of the pedigree stud dog should give you a signed Kennel Club registration form, which will contain registration details relating to the dog.

STEP 4
- Three weeks after mating, consult your vet for his advice in respect of confirming that your bitch is indeed pregnant. Besides feeling your bitch's abdomen to detect the presence of foetuses in the womb (they are about the size of a marble and strung out like a necklace), a number of different tests are available, including: radiography, ultrasound imaging, and a recently developed blood test that measures the levels of the hormone relaxin in the blood. Leave it to your vet to decide what is relevant in your particular case.

EVIDENCE OF PREGNANCY

The average weight gain in pregnant bitches from oestrus to parturition (whelping) is 36 per cent (range 20-55 per cent), the increase being most marked in the last third of pregnancy. A change in body shape is usually visible by about day 56 of pregnancy, and at the same time foetal movements may be noted. Mammary development occurs and the nipples enlarge and darken during the second half of pregnancy. Shortly before whelping, a small amount of opaque or white mucus may be noted coming from the vulva. If this becomes blood-stained, prompt veterinary assistance should be obtained.

Pedigree bitch owners frequently wish to know whether their bitches are pregnant following a planned mating, partly out of curiosity but also so that adequate plans can be made in advance of the anticipated whelping date. Generally it is sensible to consult your veterinary surgeon soon after a successful mating for advice on pregnancy diagnosis, the subsequent management of your bitch, and to confirm the likely date of whelping. Owners of mongrel bitches who think their bitch might have been accidentally mated will also need to confirm whether or not their pet is pregnant so that appropriate action can be taken.

Currently, abdominal palpation is the preferred method among vets for diagnosing pregnancy in bitches. The technique is most commonly carried out three to four weeks post-mating. In the hands of experienced veterinarians, false positives are rare, but it is difficult to be certain that a bitch is *not* pregnant. Problems are frequently encountered in certain breeds, fat animals, in bitches that tense their abdominal muscles when being felt, and in bitches who have deep chests, since the pups may be tucked away under the ribs. It is not generally wise for inexperienced people to try to feel the developing puppies since they are at a critical stage of their development at this time, and a clumsy or prolonged palpation (assessment by feeling) could damage them.

X-rays are also used on occasion in small-animal practice to confirm pregnancy, but it is not until day 45 that the foetal skeletons become visible.

Foetal heartbeats can be seen from days 20-24 of pregnancy and onwards, using the same ultrasound imaging equipment used in women. But the accuracy of the method depends very much on the equipment used, and the skill and expertise of the operator. Ultrasound can be useful to vets since it can *help* determine the number and size of the puppies and their viability. This information can be very useful when a Caesarean section is being considered.

More recently, a method of measuring the levels of the hormone relaxin present in blood samples taken from pregnant bitches has been perfected. Relaxin, which is produced by the placenta, starts to appear in the blood stream at the time the fertilised eggs become implanted in the womb – usually between days 17 and 19 post-ovulation. This test is usually carried out by vets 30 days after mating, and the result can be available in as little as 10 minutes.

FAILURE TO CONCEIVE (INFERTILITY)

There are a great number of causes of infertility in bitches including:

- Faulty mating technique or inappropriate timing of mating – these are probably the most common causes.
- Inflammation or anatomical deformity of the reproductive tract.
- Bacterial and viral infections.
- Abnormalities of the oestrous cycle, which may be associated with hypothyroidism, hormonal imbalance or poor nutrition.
- Failure to maintain adequate levels of progesterone throughout the pregnancy, possibly leading to foetal resorption or abortion.

Impotency or lack of libido in the stud dog may also be involved, including defects in spermatogenesis, hypothyroidism, inflammation of the testes, as a result of infection or trauma, and obesity.

Treatment may involve the administration of hormones, antibiotics and possibly management changes. Because infertility problems in bitches can be caused by a number of different factors, a full and rigorous veterinary investigation is required, and, in a breeding kennel, there is usually the need for an 'on site' investigation. Needless to say, this can prove both time-consuming and costly.

CHAPTER 4

CARE OF THE PREGNANT BITCH

O nce a successful mating has taken place, there is a great deal for the owner to do to ensure that the pregnancy proceeds as smoothly as possible.

DURATION OF PREGNANCY

The duration of pregnancy in the bitch has always been regarded as 63 days post-mating. However, a range of 58-68 days from the first mating to whelping is more likely to be correct, but it is worth noting that some studies have shown that the duration of pregnancy may range from 54-72 days (average 62.3 days) post-mating. This large variation is due, at least in part, to the longevity of dog spermatozoa described in Chapter Three. The *true* gestation length, that is the time from *ovulation* to *parturition* is in fact remarkably constant at 63 days (± one day). (See Figure 9.)

FEEDING

A normal, healthy bitch does not have any large increase in tissue growth during the early part of pregnancy. Most foetal growth takes place during

FIGURE 9: DURATION OF PREGNANCY IN BITCHES

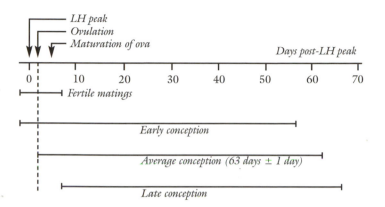

the last three weeks, and although there is considerable development of mammary and uterine tissue before this time, the need for extra nutrients and energy over and above maintenance requirements is quite small. Pregnant bitches make more efficient use of the food they eat than those that are not pregnant.

A bitch in good condition at mating will not need any special food during pregnancy as long as she receives her usual *balanced* diet. All that is necessary is a gradual increase in the total food allowance during the second half of gestation. A 15 per cent increase each week from the fifth week of pregnancy onwards is generally recommended, so that at whelping her intake is approximately 60 per cent (just less than ⅔) more than at mating. Feeding smaller, more frequent meals may be necessary during the last week or two of pregnancy.

Minerals, particularly calcium, and vitamins are present at adequate levels in all balanced mainstream prepared foods produced by reputable manufacturers, so no supplementation is required. Indeed, the over-zealous use of mineral or vitamin supplements can be wasteful and even harmful to pregnant animals. B-group vitamins are not likely to be harmful in excess, but too much cod liver oil or other sources of vitamins A and D can be damaging if used too liberally. High mineral intake does not make larger puppies or stronger bones at this stage.

It is particularly important to avoid calcium supplementation during pregnancy, as it may increase the risk of eclampsia – milk fever (see Chapter Six).

EXERCISE

A pregnant bitch needs exercise (out of doors if possible), but don't encourage 'rough-and-tumble' games, particularly in the later stages. Regular short walks should be continued right up to the whelping date, provided the bitch shows no distress and is allowed to move at her own pace.

GROOMING AND BATHING

Continue regular, thorough but gentle grooming throughout pregnancy. As the whelping date approaches, clip the hair in long-haired breeds around the rear end, so that the area around the vulva can be kept clean more easily during and after whelping, and under the abdomen to give the puppies easy access to the mammary glands. Provided regular brushing is maintained, bathing in the second half of pregnancy should be restricted to areas that clearly need it.

MEDICATION

WORMING

Bitches should be routinely wormed during pregnancy, under the guidance of your veterinary surgeon. Products containing the modern endoparasitic compound fenbendazole (which is active against the adult and larval stages of the roundworm *Toxocara canis)* can be given to help ensure that puppies are not infected with larvae while they are in the uterus or from the bitch's milk. It is recommended that pregnant bitches are dosed from day 40 of pregnancy to two days post-whelping (about 25 days in all). Control of this parasite is especially important since it can be passed on to humans, particularly children. Your vet will be happy to advise on the best course of action; new products and methods of administration are being developed continually. (For more details, see Chapter Seven.)

CONTROL OF ECTOPARASITES

Any external parasites, such as fleas or lice, should be dealt with during the first half of pregnancy by using a suitable product (see Chapter Seven). Insecticidal shampoos that are not recommended for use on puppies should not be used within three weeks of whelping.

VACCINATION

Bitches should be given regular primary and booster vaccinations before mating. However, where this has not been done, vets may advise vaccination during pregnancy. In kennels where a herpes virus infection is considered to be the cause of fading puppies, the vet may advise that the bitch is vaccinated with a recently introduced product containing canine herpes virus antigens seven to 10 days after mating and one to two weeks before whelping. Vaccination of dogs is discussed in more detail in Chapter Seven.

CONSTIPATION

If there are any signs that the bitch is experiencing difficulty in passing motions, treatment with liquid paraffin for two to three days, at a dose rate of a teaspoonful to a tablespoonful daily (according to the bitch's size), is advisable, as constipation is likely to complicate the birth of puppies. Treatment should be discontinued after a short period, otherwise the motions may become too greasy.

GENERAL MEDICATION

Medication during pregnancy should be minimal, and under veterinary guidance, because of possible adverse effects on the developing puppies.

ACCOMMODATION

Quite obviously, the type of accommodation needed for breeding bitches will be very largely dependent on the number and size of bitches used for breeding and the number of puppies that will be reared annually. This subject is considered under the headings Regular Breeders and Occasional Breeders (see below). The latter heading applies to those owners of mongrel or pedigree bitches who simply want to have a litter from their pet bitch, or who need to produce a litter as part of a 'breeding terms' commitment.

REGULAR BREEDERS

Anybody who breeds regularly (see Appendix 1) is required by law to be licensed by the Local Authority. Each Local Authority has its own set of rules and regulations governing the standard of accommodation required to house breeding stock, and the need to keep accurate records of all litters produced.

In most cases, regular breeders who have a number of breeding bitches and stud dogs keep them in purpose-built outdoor kennels. This offers the advantages of better ventilation, easier cleaning and more effective disinfection. However, it can be detrimental to the puppies' socialisation and habituation (see Chapter 8, page 109). Generally, the housing used needs to meet the standards noted below:

- The buildings must be constructed in such a manner so that they are easy to clean, preferably using impermeable materials that will not harbour dirt and infectious organisms.
- The natural and artificial lighting must be sufficient to allow good working conditions and help cleaning. There should be no dark areas.
- The buildings must be well ventilated but not draughty.
- The sleeping areas must be maintained at a suitable temperature; draughts and damp must be excluded. Heating may be provided by wall heaters specifically designed for kennels, infra-red and dull emitter lamps or heated beds. The sleeping area should be large enough to contain a raised bed of sufficient size to allow dogs and bitches to stretch out. The bedding material should be, preferably, polyester fleece or shredded paper, both of which are hygienic and warm.
- Dogs should have access to escape-proof runs, which should be paved or surfaced in such a way to allow effective cleaning and disinfection. Grass runs very quickly become fouled. Bitches with litters need to be provided with an individual sleeping area and run. Needless to say, stud dogs should be accommodated in separate runs.
- An area should be set aside in which to store and prepare food for the dogs. All food should be kept in vermin-proof containers or refrigerated where appropriate.
- It is helpful to provide a larger fenced area where dogs can be exercised while their individual accommodation is being cleaned and disinfected.
- Extra accommodation to allow the rotation of runs and for isolation purposes in the case of illness, or when new stock is introduced, can be very advantageous.

OCCASIONAL BREEDERS
Pet bitches can, of course, be accommodated in the home when they are in whelp. It is necessary simply to provide a secluded area in a suitable, quiet room for the actual whelping, and bitches should be introduced to the selected place in the last week or so of pregnancy. There are no specific regulations to observe.

KENNEL HYGIENE (FOR REGULAR BREEDERS)

CLEANLINESS
With dogs, as is the case in respect of other animals, cleanliness and with it tidiness, is fundamental to the raising of good, sound, healthy stock.

Particular attention should be paid to keeping dust levels to a minimum. All surfaces should be regularly wiped with a warm detergent solution to remove grease and organic material. Thorough cleaning before disinfection is important since this will:

• Reduce mechanically the number of infectious organisms
• Remove the layer of dirt and grease that can protect bacteria against the action of disinfectants
• Increase the efficacy of the disinfection process – some disinfectants are inactivated by organic material such as faeces and food remains.

DISINFECTION

Cleaned surfaces should be washed at least weekly with a suitable disinfectant of which there are legion. Many are active against most viruses and bacteria, and they also have effective cleaning and deodorising properties. Your vet will advise you on the most cost-effective product for your needs.

New, improved disinfectants are being continually produced, and many innovative products are marketed especially for use in kennels and have DEFRA (Department for the Environment Food and Rural Affairs) approval for that indication.

Advice on which disinfectant will be most suitable for any particular situation can be obtained from your veterinary surgery, a good pet shop or pet superstore. It is most important to follow precisely the instructions given with the product. In this context, too, it is worth noting that the efficacy of disinfectants is generally increased when they are freshly made.

CHAPTER 5

WHELPING

Whelping is a natural process for the bitch, and most births take place with little complication. However, it is vital that the breeder makes adequate provision for the whelping process and that steps are in place to deal with possible complications.

WHELPING FACILITIES

LARGE-/MEDIUM-SIZED BREEDS
Bitches should be provided with a quiet, dry, draught-free area where they can be carefully watched during whelping, with a minimum of disturbance. Regular breeders of large breeds generally keep their breeding stock in outside kennels but whelp and rear their puppies initially in the home. A quiet room in the house, away from distractions, will serve well. In the case of pet bitches, their own bed can be used as a whelping box provided it is large enough. However, a more suitable box for whelping can be made of hardboard with three high sides and a lower front. A rectangular or square box is preferable to a circular bed or basket, as puppies can find protection in the corners when the bitch

lies down. In the case of large bitches, 'pig rails' placed along the sides of the whelping box can provide extra protection for the puppies and should prevent a clumsy bitch from lying on her pups.

There should be enough room for the mother to turn around and to accommodate her litter up to the age of four to five weeks.

Whelping boxes should be constructed of material that can be easily cleaned and disinfected. Disposable whelping boxes have been made available recently. These have the advantage that they won't harbour any infection or parasites and don't take up a lot of room because they can be folded. After use they can be burnt.

The whelping box should be situated in a quiet place, since bitches do not appreciate being overly disturbed during whelping and in the first few days after giving birth.

For an average-sized bitch (30 lb/13.5 kg), the sides of the box should be about 8 inches (20 cm) high and the front about 2 inches (5 cm) high.

SMALL BREEDS

With regard to whelping accommodation, small breeds have slightly different requirements, as litters are generally raised entirely in the house until they are ready to home. Consequently, they have somewhat of a head start when it comes to habituation and socialisation.

Small bitches can be accommodated in a strong cardboard box, of adequate size, which can be replaced when wet or dirty.

The construction of the whelping box also differs from that required for large breeds, as it is customary in the case of small breeds to use a box that can be completely enclosed. Again, the box should be constructed of a material that can be easily cleaned and disinfected. Purpose-designed boxes are becoming available, which are made from plastic or cardboard; these offer several obvious advantages. While the actual whelping is taking place, the box should be completely opened up to enable the bitch to be watched closely from above and so that she can be given help if necessary.

ALL BREEDS

It is very important that bitches become accustomed to their maternity quarters well before the expected event: about two weeks should suffice in most cases.

The whelping box should be placed in a room where it is readily accessible, away from constant comings and goings and other disturbances, and where the litter is going to be brought up for the first two weeks. Later it will need to be moved to a situation, usually the kitchen, where the puppies will experience the noises and sights of everyday living so that they can become properly habituated and socialised from an early age. There should be easy access to the outside world so that house-training can commence (see Chapter Eight).

As the puppies become older, they will need to be accommodated in an enclosed run, which serves the purpose of allowing them to see and hear everything that is going on in the household, and at the same time keeping them out of harm's way.

TOY BREEDS

Toy breeds can be very sensitive when whelping, so it is important that the whelping box is situated in a calm, warm area away from the main 'traffic' in the house and places where people congregate.

BEDDING

Newspaper makes excellent bedding, as it is clean, warm, easily available and expendable. Blankets or sheets should be changed frequently and washed thoroughly before re-use. Easily washed bedding that can be replaced frequently when soiled is a necessity.

Modern synthetic materials that allow fluids to soak through are extremely useful, practical and hygienic. Polyester fleece is especially comfortable for the puppies, as the surface is always warm and dry. It has the added advantage that it gives young pups something to grip as they move around the whelping box.

HEATING

An additional heat source is the most important matter to consider. Many newborn puppies die of hypothermia because, for the first few days of life, they can't shiver and are unable to regulate their own body temperature. The ambient temperature should be kept comfortably high, and a source of conductible heat should be provided so that puppies can maintain their body temperature. Examples of suitable heat sources are:

- Central heating turned up enough to provide an ambient temperature of 75-78 degrees Fahrenheit (24-26 C).
- Infra-red and dull emitter lamps at the recommended height.
- Heated electrical pads to provide contact heat – see below.
- Purpose-built whelping boxes with heated bases.
- A slim metal electrically heated pad is not too expensive to buy and could easily save a puppy's life. When the puppies have left, these pads can be placed under trays of seedlings to warm the soil for

germination! Hot-water bottles and the newer microwavable heat pads can be useful initially, but they are not very practical in the long term, as they cool relatively quickly and need replacing frequently.

With small and toy breeds, special care must be taken to ensure that the ambient temperature in the box and the whelping area is constant at no lower than 75 degrees F (24 C), and even as high as 80 F (27 C), as these breeds are especially at risk from hypothermia due to their relatively large surface area in comparison to their weight.

LIGHTING
Lighting should be kept subdued, as this keeps the bitch calm and won't damage the young puppies' eyes when they start to open at around two weeks of age.

PREPARATIONS

WHELPING ROOM
For the whelping, you will need to select a corner in a quiet, secluded room, which will allow you and any assistants easy access to the whelping box. The room should be kept at around 75-80 F (24-27 C); it should contain comfortable seating (you may need to spend many hours in there!), and a table for the equipment that you will need to keep to hand. You will need washing facilities, towels and soap, so that you can clean your hands between procedures. Set aside a clear area where you can keep a book in which to record events. A mobile phone is a must these days!

EQUIPMENT
Ideally the following items should be prepared a week or two before the due date:
- A note of your vet's telephone number and possibly that of a taxi company in case you need transport in a hurry.
- A small cardboard box, with towelling-covered hot-water bottle, an electrically heated pad or a microwaveable corn bag, to receive the puppies should you have to remove them from the bitch temporarily while she is whelping.
- A good supply of old newspapers, as well as kitchen paper, cotton wool and gauze swabs. Whelping produces large amounts of fluid!
- Nail brush, soap and towels for washing hands.
- Pieces of towelling for drying the puppies.
- Notebook and pen to record the times the puppies are born, the

interval between births and other relevant observations. The puppies will need to be described or marked in some way so their position in the birth sequence can be identified later (see Record-keeping, page 64)

- Scales for weighing the puppies at birth and afterwards.
- A good torch so that you can observe your bitch closely in case she needs to go outside to urinate.
- Antiseptic solution. Your vet will advise the latest most suitable product.
- Plastic sacks for soiled paper and other waste materials (including afterbirths).
- A small vial (bottle) of the respiratory stimulant Dopram V can be a useful standby for regular, experienced breeders. This product can be obtained from veterinary surgeons, some pet shops or even by mail order (see dog press or the internet).

ASSISTANCE
Line someone up to be available should you need help. Generally, though, you are better off without any 'on-lookers' present at the birth. You will need a car at your disposal so that your bitch can be taken to the surgery if the vet feels it is advisable. Transporting the bitch is a two-person job, as she may produce a puppy on the journey there, or back!

NORMAL WHELPING
The events that take place immediately before and during parturition have been described by many authors. The description that follows is a compilation of the major observations made and our own experience.

INITIATING EVENTS
The precise mechanisms that initiate whelping have not been clearly identified in bitches. However, it is thought that the start of the whelping process is brought about by a series of hormonal changes, particularly falling progesterone and rising oestrogen levels in the blood. This results in the production of prostaglandins by the developing young and their placentae. Prostaglandins, it is thought, together with the hormone relaxin in the mother, bring about relaxation of the pelvis, uterine contractions and abdominal straining both directly, and by causing the hormone oxytocin to be released from the pituitary gland in the brain. This whole 'cascade' of events is probably triggered by rising cortisone production by the puppies, as their hormonal system matures at the end of the gestation period. Thus, it seems that the puppies initiate their own birth!

SIGNS OF IMMINENT WHELPING

While the hormonal changes described above are taking place, the bitch's temperature, normally 101-102 degrees F (38-39 C), drops to 97-99 F (37-38 C), and this is frequently taken by breeders as an indication that whelping will occur within the next 24 hours. However, it should be noted that the body temperature of pregnant bitches is already about 0.5 F lower during the last week of pregnancy than is normal for non-pregnant, adult bitches.

During the last two to three days before parturition, bitches commonly show characteristic behavioural signs, such as seeking darkened places and solitude, restlessness and nest-making. The presence or absence of milk is too variable to be a reliable sign of impending parturition. Just before whelping, the vagina frequently becomes somewhat swollen and a slight vaginal discharge may be seen. Bitches frequently refuse food for a day or two before whelping.

Overall, it should be remembered that giving birth is a natural process and that interference is best kept to a minimum.

LABOUR

Classically, labour is divided into three stages:
- First stage: relaxation and dilation of the cervix
- Second stage: the production of the young
- Third stage: the expulsion of the placentae (afterbirths).

In animals like bitches, who produce more than one offspring, the mother will fluctuate between the second and third stages as each newborn is produced.

FIRST-STAGE LABOUR

During this stage, which lasts on average four hours (but up to 36 hours in bitches producing their first litter), the cervix relaxes and dilates, the bitch becomes more restless and nervous; she shivers, pants and may vomit. Many bitches will shred their beds, possibly as a reaction to pain. Milk, which may be expressed from the teats during the last few weeks of pregnancy, is let down more plentifully during this stage.

SECOND-STAGE LABOUR

This stage is characterised by strong contractions of the womb and by visible abdominal straining. Between contractions the bitch will lick her vulval region, especially once the waters break. The bitch usually lies on her side and continues to pant heavily between contractions; this is particularly so in the short-nosed breeds. Toy breeds often remain standing.

Once a puppy's head or pelvis enters the bitch's pelvis (as many as 40 per cent of puppies present posteriorly – see Figure 10), strong *abdominal* straining is stimulated. The duration of this stage is extremely variable between individual bitches, and between the delivery of puppies within a single litter. As a general rule, whelping bitches should be examined by a vet if the first puppy does not appear after one to two hours of persistent abdominal straining. Certainly no more than three to four hours should be allowed to elapse after the start of regular *uterine* contractions and the delivery of the first puppy before a veterinary investigation is carried out. This is because separation of the afterbirths is likely to occur by that time, and the remaining puppies' lives could be threatened.

FIGURE 10: NORMAL BIRTH PRESENTATIONS

ANTERIOR PRESENTATION

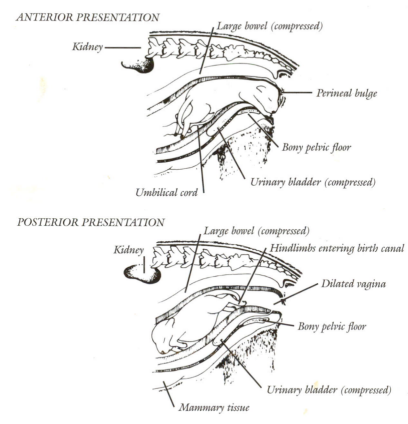

POSTERIOR PRESENTATION

The interval between births is similarly variable with bitches alternating between stages two and three of labour and periods of rest. Second and subsequent puppies should be produced with no more than 30 minutes of abdominal straining; seek prompt veterinary attention if non-productive abdominal straining persists for more than half an hour. Rest periods of more than three to four hours between bouts of uterine straining should be regarded as abnormal. It is not uncommon for a large litter to take up to 24 hours to be produced – and possibly even longer.

Bitches who are good mothers will clean and suckle the puppies between successive births and it is probably better to allow this to occur. Taking the puppies away as they are born and returning them only when whelping has ended can upset the bitch.

THIRD-STAGE LABOUR
During this stage, the afterbirths are expelled. Puppies may be born with the membranes intact, or they may be born attached by the umbilical cord with the placenta remaining in the bitch's genital tract. In the latter case, when the cord is broken the placenta will be expelled separately, either before, with or after subsequent births. If the afterbirth has not come away with the puppy, or if the afterbirth and the puppy emerge together, the umbilical cord will need to be *torn* to separate the puppy. On no account should the cord be cut with sharp scissors or a scalpel blade, nor should the cord be pulled against the puppy's abdomen (see Figure 11).

FIGURE 11: BREAKING THE UMBILICAL CORD

Correct

Incorrect

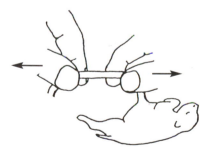
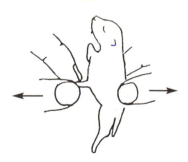

It is a matter of personal preference whether or not bitches are allowed to eat the afterbirths; it has been suggested that the ingested placental hormones may help the womb to return to normal after whelping and stimulate milk production. It is probably unwise, however, to let a bitch eat all the afterbirths in the case of large litters, since that could cause an intestinal upset, particularly diarrhoea.

The only sign that whelping has ended is that the bitch will relax and start nursing her puppies contentedly.

DIFFICULT BIRTH (DYSTOCIA)

INCIDENCE AND GENERAL ADVICE

In as many as 25-40 per cent of whelpings, there is a 'hold up', which can lead to the death of one or more puppies. In essence, the cause of such a problem lies either with the bitch or with the puppies themselves. Thus, dystocia can be associated with primary or secondary inertia of the womb, or oversized or malpositioned puppies.

Whatever you think is the cause of dystocia, veterinary assistance should always be sought – no attempt should be made to try to establish a puppy's presentation (whether it is coming head or hind feet first). Never, ever attempt to correct the position of a puppy not presented normally. The only assistance that may be given is when puppies are halfway delivered. In that case *gentle* traction downwards and backwards may be applied (see Figure 12 – for details, see The Breeder's Role During Stage 2, page 57).

FIGURE 12: ASSISTING THE BIRTH

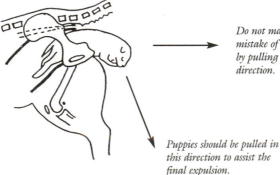

Do not make the common mistake of assisting birth by pulling in this direction.

Puppies should be pulled in this direction to assist the final expulsion.

Finally, it should be noted that many of the causes of dystocia are inherited. Breeders often say that a poor whelper, or poor mother, will give birth to bitch puppies who, in turn, are poor whelpers and mothers. The wisdom of breeding again from such animals should, therefore, always be questioned and discussed with a veterinary surgeon.

UTERINE INTERTIA (DELAYED PARTURITION)

Uterine inertia, failure of the womb to contract normally, is probably the most common and worrying cause of dystocia in bitches, and always requires veterinary attention. The cause is not entirely clear, but mechanical, physical, genetic and hormonal factors are doubtless involved, possibly acting together. Two types of uterine inertia are recognised:

- **Primary uterine inertia:** In such cases, the bitch fails to show any signs of impending whelping, or fails to progress from stage one to stage two. Vets usually advise that a Caesarean section is needed without delay if live puppies are to be produced. Injections of the hormone oxytocin have very little or no effect. *The presence of copious amounts of dark green fluid in bitches not showing signs of first stage of labour indicates the need for veterinary help and usually a Caesarean section.*

  Usually in cases of partial primary uterine inertia, drugs to stimulate contractions, most commonly oxytocin, are given by vets in small, repeated doses by intramuscular or intravenous injection. Oxytocin injections should always be given under close supervision because the hormone can be harmful if administered incorrectly or in the wrong situation.

- **Secondary uterine inertia:** This is most frequently due to exhaustion of the muscles of the womb and follows protracted straining to deliver a puppy that is lodged in the birth canal, or in the delivery of large litters. Unless large numbers of puppies remain, most vets will give an injection of oxytocin, which will often succeed in bringing about contractions sufficiently powerful to complete the birth of pups. If that is not the case, a Caesarean section will be required, as is the case if the medication fails to re-establish uterine contractions.

OVERSIZED PUPPIES

One or more of the puppies may be simply too big to go through the bitch's pelvis, or the puppies may be of normal size but the bitch's pelvis is too small (relative oversize). The former problem can be the result of a mating with too large a dog; the latter can be congenital (the bitch having been born with an unusually narrow pelvis), or the result of an earlier fracture, leading to a narrowing of the passage. Virtually without exception, these cases can only be resolved by carrying out a Caesarean section; you must be prepared to be guided by your veterinary surgeon.

MALPOSITION

Puppies can be born quite naturally whether they are presented head or hind legs first. However, problems can arise if the fore legs or head are bent backwards or to one side as the puppies enter the birth canal. In the case of puppies being born backwards, problems can arise if the hind

FIGURE 13: PUPPY MALPRESENTATION AT BIRTH

DOWNWARD FLEXION OF THE HEAD

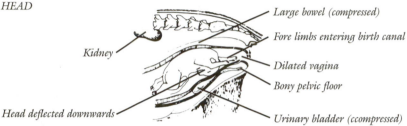

Large bowel (compressed)

Fore limbs entering birth canal

Kidney

Dilated vagina

Bony pelvic floor

Head deflected downwards

Urinary bladder (ccompressed)

SIDEWAYS DEVIATION OF THE HEAD

Large bowel (compressed)

Presenting shoulder

Kidney

Dilated vagina

Bony pelvic floor

Head, neck and fore limb deflected

Urinary bladder (compressed)

BREECH PRESENTATION

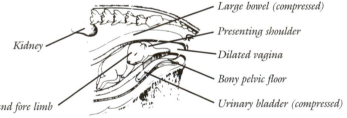

Large bowel (compressed)

Buttocks and tail entering birth canal

Kidney

Dilated vagina

Bony pelvic floor

Urinary bladder (compressed)

legs are bent forwards (breech presentation; see Figure 13). It is usually impossible to correct the puppy's position, the bitch is inevitably exhausted, and usually there are more pups following. Therefore, your vet will have little choice but to carry out a Caesarean operation.

THE BREEDER'S ROLE

AS THE DAY APPROACHES

The general rule is that if the bitch appears fit and well and is eating, no special action need be taken for two to three days after the estimated whelping date i.e. on average 62.3 days post-mating (see Chapter Four). Always note the dates of mating very carefully to avoid mistakes in estimating the whelping date. If there is any vomiting, maintained loss of appetite, excessive thirst or vaginal discharge without other signs of birth, a vet should be asked to examine the animal without delay. A green-stained vulval discharge *before* uterine contractions or straining starts is a significant warning sign that all is not well; seek veterinary help promptly. Note, however, that as whelping progresses and as the puppies are being born, a green-stained discharge is quite normal. If more than three days elapse after the due date, professional help needs to be sought in any case.

DURING STAGE 1

- The beginning of the first stage is often ill-defined. As noted earlier, bitches may refuse a meal, and, in some cases, vomiting occurs so that straining during the second stage is easier. The bitch may be restless and desire company during this period, but as the second stage approaches, she is likely to be more settled alone or in the presence of just the breeder.
- Supervision should be unobtrusive and it is usually sufficient for the bitch to know that someone she trusts is at hand.
- Most bitches will keep themselves and the whelping area clean by licking up the fluid produced at this stage. In some cases, you may need to assist by mopping up.

DURING STAGE 2

- The second stage of labour begins when abdominal straining proper occurs, and it is as well to make a note of the time this starts. If the first puppy has not appeared after an hour of such regular, strong straining, professional advice must be sought so that bitches are not left straining for more than two hours, as this will leave them exhausted for the job ahead.

- Delivering the puppy's head requires the greatest effort by the bitch, and sometimes contractions are not sufficient for the final expulsion of the puppy's chest and the rest of its body. In this case, backwards and downward traction may be exerted away from the horizontal plane of the spine (see Figure 12). Force should not be exerted, only firm, gentle traction, preferably as the bitch herself strains. Be prepared for those bitches who produce puppies without you being aware that stage 1 has even started!
- The membranes forming the sac around the puppy do not always rupture at birth. In the case of puppies born in an intact sac, it is important to tear open the sac with your fingers. You will need to clear the puppy's nose and mouth quickly, with a small piece of gauze or towelling, so that it can breathe. The bitch usually does all this, but if she does not, you will need to be prepared to help, promptly.

DURING STAGE 3
- The afterbirths are usually expelled either with each puppy as it is born, or just afterwards. It is useful to count them to make sure each is accounted for. If the puppy is born with the afterbirth still attached, the cord can be broken by *tearing* it with clean fingernails, taking care not to pull on the puppy's abdomen. Do *not* cut the cord with scissors or a sharp knife as this can result in excessive blood loss. About two inches (5 cm) of cord should be left attached to the puppy; this will soon shrivel up and drop off – it is better to leave it longer rather than shorter. (See Figure 11.)
- After each birth, the bitch will spend a lot of time licking the newborn puppy, which will dry it and stimulate breathing. If she fails to do this, each puppy will need to be dried firmly and quite vigorously with a piece of towelling, especially if it is not crying and does not seem to be breathing freely.
- The bitch should not be left straining on second or subsequent puppies for more than 30-60 minutes without result. Contact your vet after no more than 30 minutes' unproductive strong and frequent straining to allow him or her to see the bitch in good time.
- During whelping, puppies may be left with the bitch, unless they make her agitated. If this happens, the newborn puppies should be kept in a warm, dry box. They may be allowed to feed from the bitch whenever she is not straining or restless.
- Newly born puppies are unable to control their body temperature effectively because they can't shiver, and chilling is rapidly fatal. A hot-water bottle wrapped in a towel, or other means of contact heat in the box, will ensure that they are kept at the proper temperature. Be

careful to avoid overheating with overhead heaters. Care must also be taken to exclude draughts.

- Small amounts of fluid may be offered to the bitch to drink between the birth of successive puppies. A glucose/milk/water mixture is suitable to replace fluid lost during whelping. The fluid voided by bitches during whelping is usually green/brown in colour due to the breakdown of blood in the placenta. This colour is quite normal, and, as noted earlier, is not a cause for concern.

- It is not easy to tell when a bitch has finished whelping, although any remaining puppies may be felt in the abdomen by careful examination by an experienced veterinary surgeon. It is advisable to ask a vet to examine the bitch within 24 hours after whelping appears to have finished; you may be asked to take the bitch and her litter to the surgery. If all has gone well, some vets may advise that it is not necessary and that even the slight risk of infection associated with a trip to the surgery is best avoided.

- The size of the average first litter varies according to breed. It could be as few as one to three puppies for a Miniature Poodle to as much as eight to 10 for a Setter or a Boxer. Be prepared for a long attendance in the case of larger breeds.

- Some bitches are very possessive and will not leave their litter after birth to pass urine. The easiest way to get a stubborn bitch to go outside is to remove a puppy from the litter and take it out, taking care not to chill it (and beware of being bitten by a possessive bitch). Most bitches are approachable by a person they know and trust.

- Finally, remember that, in all cases, the fewer people around during the whole whelping process and immediately after, the better it is for the bitch.

WHELPING: STEP BY STEP

STEP 1
About a week or two before the due date, move your bitch into her whelping quarters and let her sleep in the box you have prepared in which she will give birth.

STEP 2
As the day approaches, check that you have all the equipment you will need for the whelping itself. Ensure that anyone you have asked to help is on standby, and tell your veterinary surgeon of the imminent event. Make sure that your own diary is clear.

STEP 3

Observe your bitch closely and regularly, and look especially for any changes in behaviour. Squeeze the bitch's nipples gently to check for the presence of milk. Examine the vulva for swelling and for any discharge.

STEP 4

Once your bitch becomes nervous or restless, or begins to circle, paw at the nest, shiver and pant, you will know that you are 'on you way'. Note that all bitches do not show all the signs noted above – and some may even produce a puppy without any warning whatsoever! Either way don't panic, keep calm and remember that, to bitches, giving birth is a completely natural event. *Note the time: the clock is running.*

STEP 5

As soon as you see any abdominal straining, *note the time again* and start to check the interval between straining efforts.

Don't make any attempt to hold or place the bitch in any particular position – she knows what's most comfortable, relatively speaking!

The imminent arrival of a puppy is generally indicated by the bitch turning to lick her vulva, and the appearance of a copious amount of fluid. Don't worry if you don't see any sign of straining – as long as a puppy arrives, that's quite okay. Just before the puppy is born you may observe the so-called 'crowning' – a firm swelling between the vulva and the anus, which pushes the bitch's tail upwards. This is perfectly normal and occurs when the puppy, still within its sac, is in the final part of the birth canal.

STEP 6

If no puppies present or arrive after one hour (maximum two hours) of strong abdominal straining by the bitch, call the vet. Be prepared to take your bitch to the surgery. It may be that all she needs is the help of an oxytocin injection and/or a calcium injection, but be prepared also for the fact that the litter may need to be delivered by Caesarean section.

STEP 7

Many puppies will be born in an intact sac full of fluid, making it difficult to tell whether it has been born head or hind legs first – not that it matters! In this case, initially leave the bitch to sort things out for herself. She will lick hard at the membrane surrounding the puppy and, in doing so, she will open the sac. She will then begin to lick the puppy vigorously. If it cries, you will know she has been successful and all is well – make a cup of tea! If the puppy does not cry or begin to move, or if the bitch fails to break the sac, pick it up; be careful, it will be slippery. Use a piece of cloth if necessary. Open the sac yourself with your fingers and nails. Break the cord by shredding it between the thumb and finger of each hand (see Figure 11). If necessary, use your thumb nail to fray and tear the cord. As mentioned earlier, *do not* cut it with sharp scissors or a knife, since that can lead to excessive loss of blood.

Clear the puppy's mouth of any mucus and rub the puppy firmly with a piece of towelling. If it cries, all is well, and you can relax and return the puppy to the bitch so that she can complete the job. If rubbing does not stimulate the puppy to cry, take it in your hand, supporting its head with your fingers, and swing it at arm's length like a pendulum to remove any fluid from its mouth and throat. Keep trying this, and rubbing the puppy intermittently, until you meet with success. At this stage, experienced breeders could try placing a drop of Dopram V, a respiratory stimulant, under the puppy's tongue. This can sometimes work like a miracle. But do follow the instructions carefully. You may have to persevere and have patience. Be prepared to give up if you are not successful after 10-15 minutes. The chances are that the puppy died in the womb and was 'still-born'.

Once you are happy that the pup is breathing freely, make a note of what you have done and the time. Mark the puppy, or write down a description of it, so that you can recognise it again; note its sex and weigh it. You should also, of course, identify and weigh all puppies as they are born, whether they arrive naturally or with assistance. If you have a Polaroid or digital camera, consider taking a photograph of each puppy to supplement your description. Alternatively, marking them with different coloured felt pens is probably the best method, unless they have very distinctive markings, which you can note. With black puppies it may prove helpful to cut off a patch of hair in different places.

STEP 8

If the sac ruptures as the puppy is being born, you will see either its head appearing first or its hind legs. Either way, it's perfectly normal. Incidentally, hind feet first is *not* a breech presentation; that occurs when the hind legs are bent forward and the puppy's 'bottom' appears first (see Figure 13). Give the bitch time to expel the puppy herself, head or hind legs first. If she is not successful after straining a few times, you may apply very gentle traction downwards (away from the spine) and backwards (see Figure 12) *as she strains*. Because newborn puppies are slippery, you may need to hold the head or feet as shown in Figure 14, possibly with the aid of a piece of gauze. If the puppy does not emerge fully after you have pulled gently for two to three minutes, *phone your vet*. Once you have delivered the puppy in this way, you should proceed as noted in Step 7 by breaking the cord and rubbing, and swinging the puppy if that proves necessary.

FIGURE 14: ASSISTING THE FINAL EXPULSION OF A PUPPY

TRACTION BY THE HEAD   *TRACTION BY THE HIND LEGS*

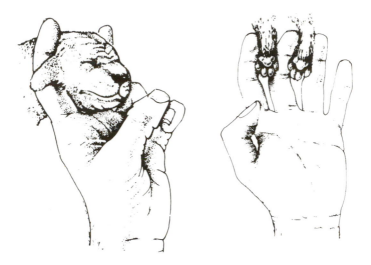

STEP 9

Be prepared to repeat Steps 7 and 8 at one- to two-hour intervals, but possibly more frequently. There is great variation in how quickly subsequent puppies are born. Provided the bitch is resting quietly and not straining, you can relax and continue your tea drinking! But be vigilant and keep your eye on the clock.

However, if your bitch starts to strain unproductively for more than half an hour, *call your vet*. Don't be tempted to put your fingers in the bitch's vulva to feel what goes on – you will do no good at all. Deviation of the head or breech presentation can lead to dystocia. It is the job of a veterinary surgeon to determine the nature of the malpresentation, or any other cause of a hold-up in the whelping sequence.

It is okay to let earlier arrivals suck from the bitch's nipples as long as she is not concerned. However, if she gets too restless or agitated as another puppy is about to arrive, take the puppies away and put them in the heated box that you have prepared earlier.

In between each arrival, offer your bitch a drink; she may or may not want it – don't worry if she refuses to drink and certainly don't force her to take any fluid.

STEP 10

Usually the afterbirths will come with, or follow, closely after each puppy as it is born. If this does not happen, don't worry. It helps to keep count of the number of afterbirths you see for peace or mind, but don't be concerned if one or two are missing. They will almost certainly appear later – unless the bitch has eaten them when you were not looking! It is fine for your bitch to eat the afterbirths, but in the case of large litters, it is better not to let her eat them all. If your bitch shows no interest in eating an afterbirth, simply remove it and dispose of it yourself.

STEP 11

Your only indication that whelping is over is that the bitch will relax and let the puppies suck. All you have to do now is to praise her, and offer her food and drink. Note the time and check that all your records are complete. Give your bitch the chance to go outside, but if she is comfortable and not worried, don't force her. This is the time for you to examine the puppies carefully, but briefly, to ensure that they are intact, have no obvious deformation (such as a cleft palate), and, importantly, that they are dry. They should *all* be suckling and appear contented. There is no need to do anything with the umbilical cords, the bitch will shorten them by nibbling at them if *she* considers it necessary. Finally, ensure that the room temperature is adequate, around 75-78 F (23.5-25.5 C), check there are no draughts, and look to see if the heated pad (if you are using one) is working properly.

STEP 12

A celebratory drink is now in order! But do make a note to call your vet to arrange for him to see your bitch and her litter within the next 12 to 24 hours or so. Some vets may decide that a house call is appropriate, but, in most cases, you will be advised to take your bitch to the surgery so that he or she can check that all's well. Be guided by the vet about whether or not to take the puppies with you when you go to the surgery. If you do leave the litter at home, it is best to wait until they have just had a meal (sucked) and are lying contentedly. Make sure that they will be warm all the time you are away. Try not to be gone for longer than absolutely necessary, and leave someone in charge to ensure that all is well at home.

A veterinary examination of the litter is helpful to check that the pups are fit, well and have no obvious imperfections (such as umbilical hernias, cleft palates and the like), but the vet may decide to leave that until later – possibly until the dew claws are removed, and docking (if required) is carried out, within a few days or so. Note that docking is a very contentious issue, and many vets will not carry out this procedure these days.

CAESAREAN SECTION

If a Caesarean – removal of the young from the uterus under general anaesthesia – becomes necessary after some of the puppies have been born, they should be kept in a warm covered box while the bitch is taken to the surgery for the operation. They will come to no harm without food for a few hours.

Modern anaesthetics mean that the bitch will awaken virtually as soon as the operation is completed. Pups born by Caesarean section may be somewhat less active because of the transmission of the anaesthetic to them, and it may take a little longer to get the bitch to accept them and for the puppies to start sucking. But, generally, Caesarean litters usually thrive quite normally.

The fact that the bitch has a surgical wound between the line of her teats, or possibly on her flank, does not usually prevent her from nursing the litter normally. The wound will usually have healed by the time the sutures are due to be removed, about a week later. The wound should, of course, be kept clean and dry; your veterinary surgeon will advise if any further action is needed.

RECORD-KEEPING

The importance of keeping an accurate record of all the events occurring before, during and immediately after whelping is frequently not recognised. Detailed records, including dates and time intervals, are of great help should veterinary assistance be needed, and could lead to more effective – and possibly less expensive – treatment. The information can also be of great help should the bitch be mated again and produce another litter.

Comprehensive notes concerning the progress of each puppy in the litter, particularly in respect of weight changes, can also prove to be very valuable.

Experienced, regular breeders will keep separate full details relating to each dog and bitch in their care. The records should note such facts as:

- Date of birth and details relating to the sire and dam.
- Dates of primary and booster vaccinations, including the name of the product(s) used.
- Dates when worming treatments have been given – again noting the name of the product(s) used.
- Details and dates of any illnesses suffered and the medication given.
- Dates when the bitch is in season, pregnant or false pregnancy, together with details of any anomalies of the oestrous cycle.
- A note of the birth weight and the result of subsequent regular weighings.
- A record of feeding routines and products used. Note particularly the dates when any major diet changes were made and products used.

CHAPTER 6

WHELPING AFTERCARE

The best indication that all is well after whelping is that the bitch is eating well, spending most of her time contentedly allowing her puppies to suck, and cleaning up after them. However, as noted previously, it is sensible to get your veterinary surgeon to check and for you to be aware of the tell-tale signs of post-whelping complications.

MEDICAL MATTERS

VETERINARY EXAMINATION
The day after whelping, ask your veterinary surgeon to examine your bitch, to check that the uterus is empty, and that there is no sign of infection or problem with the mammary glands. Don't forget to tell him if you think one or more afterbirths might be left in the womb. Most vets will give an injection of the hormone oxytocin during this examination, to ensure that the uterus contracts down promptly and properly, and that all its contents are expelled. If the whelping was protracted, or manual assistance was needed, a course of antibiotics may be prescribed to prevent the possibility of bacterial infection.

METRITIS (INFLAMMATION OF THE LINING OF THE WOMB)

You should keep a close watch for signs of illness in your bitch during the entire lactation period, but especially in the first four to 10 days post-whelping. A greenish discharge from the vulva is normal for 24 hours, followed by a brownish-red bloody discharge, which continues, in diminishing amounts, for about three to four weeks. The amount of this discharge is greater in large litters. If the discharge become black and foul-smelling, seek veterinary help *at once*. Metritis is usually the result of a bacterial infection occurring after whelping. It may be associated with trauma or retained afterbirths. Treatment usually involves the administration of antibiotics.

MASTITIS (INFLAMMATION OF THE MAMMARY GLANDS)

Check the bitch's mammary glands and nipples daily. The glands should not be hot or over-distended (although early in lactation they may be quite enlarged), and the nipples should not be cracked. You should be able to express small amounts of milk quite easily. Swollen, hot mammary glands (and possibly blood-stained milk) are indicative of mastitis, and prompt veterinary treatment is required. If you have any doubts in this connection, it is always best to seek veterinary help because if the bitch becomes feverish and refuses to eat, her milk will soon dry up and you will be left with the onerous task of hand-rearing the puppies. Treatment invariably involves the administration of antibiotics, and possibly the application of hot fomentations (meaning the use of warm lotions, usually salt water, to relieve pain) on the affected glands.

ECLAMPSIA (LACTATION TETARY)

Eclampsia is caused by low levels of calcium, and possibly glucose, in the blood stream. The condition usually occurs soon after whelping and is characterised by restlessness, panting, nervousness and collapse. *Very prompt veterinary attention is needed if the bitch is to be saved; this is indeed a true veterinary emergency.* It is worthy of note that this condition can be associated with over supplementation with calcium during pregnancy. Intravenous injections of calcium and glucose given by a veterinary surgeon usually result in a 'miraculous' cure.

AGALACTIA (FAILURE TO PRODUCE MILK)

Characteristically, the presenting signs of this condition are a litter of restless, crying and obviously hungry puppies, together with finding that no milk can be expressed from the teats. The cause of the condition is often unclear, but it may be the result of an hormonal imbalance, stress, fever, or in association with mastitis. Massaging the mammary glands can be of help in mild cases, but usually veterinary assistance is required to identify the cause so that specific treatment can be given. Bitches that have developed this condition are best retired from breeding in the future.

CARE OF PUPPIES: WEEKS 1-2

GENERAL CARE
The puppies should spend most of their time happily feeding from their mother or sleeping. If that is not the case, seek veterinary advice.

Dew claw removal (and docking where appropriate) is carried out when the puppies are around three days old, and veterinary advice should be sought if this is to be done. Occasional pedigree breeders should seek advice on this matter from the breeder of their bitch or from their veterinary surgeon.

Puppies will usually open their eyes when they are about 10 to 12 days old. Their ear canal will open when they are about two weeks old. Avoid the use of bright lights and keep noise levels down at this time. Any mucous discharge from the eyes should be removed gently, using a wet cotton wool swab. Consult your vet if you are worried at all in this connection, and certainly if the discharge contains pus and/or is persistent.

FADING PUPPIES (FADING PUPPY COMPLEX/NEONATAL MORTALITY)
This is a major problem that can cause a lot of concern, worry, and loss of revenue, particularly to regular breeders. The condition is therefore discussed at some length below.

DEFINITION
Puppies who are apparently healthy at birth but who fail to thrive and die before they reach 14 days of age.

CAUSES
The condition may be associated with the following factors acting alone or together:
- **Infectious agents:** (a) bacteria, particularly ß haemolytic streptococci (BHS) and *Escherichia coli (E.coli)*, but possibly brucella species and anaerobic organisms
  (b) *Toxoplasma gondii*
  (c) Viruses, particularly Canine Adenovirus (CAV-1) and Canine

Herpes virus
- **Hypothermia:** low body temperature
- **Bad mothering:** cannibalism and crushing
- **Dystocia:** difficult birth
- **Congenital defects:** e.g. cleft palate, absence of an anus
- **Parasites:** particularly *Toxocara canis* (roundworm) infection
- **Poor nutrition of the dam:** possibly too little protein, vitamin A or K deficiency, or inappropriate fat content in the diet.

SIGNS

Affected puppies are generally vigorous and appear healthy at birth and suck avidly for the first 24 hours. Thereafter, they become progressively weaker and make only feeble attempts to suck. They lose weight, are restless and may cry continually. They often have cramp-like muscle spasms. Occasionally, the production of blood-stained faeces and urine precedes death. Not all littermates are necessarily affected, and fading puppies may or may not be produced in subsequent litters. The signs shown by fading puppies are much the same regardless of the cause; essentially they all look the same. It is important not to fall into the trap of thinking that the condition does not exist because one or more of the signs mentioned here is not seen.

TREATMENT

The treatment of fading puppies is generally unrewarding. However, it does make sense to seek veterinary help, since, in some cases, medication (such as the administration of an antibiotic and/or fluids) may be of help in affected puppies and possibly in littermates to prevent them fading too. The bitch herself may also benefit from some medication. In some cases, it may be necessary to remove the puppies from the bitch and to feed them artificially, at least temporarily. The provision, under veterinary supervision, of an oxygen-enriched atmosphere for affected puppies to breathe can be advantageous in some cases.

Puppies suffering from hypothermia should be re-warmed gently; carrying them close to the human body by placing them in the pocket of a loose garment is one useful way of warming puppies gently. Too rapid re-heating can be counterproductive.

In breeding kennels, the bodies of puppies should *not* be discarded before seeking veterinary help, since a post-mortem examination can be extremely useful in establishing the cause of the problem. Dead puppies retained for examination should be kept cool, possibly in a refrigerator (+4 degrees C) but not frozen, since that precludes an histological examination.

PREVENTION
If a pet bitch produces a litter of fading puppies, it is probably sensible not to have her mated again. The preventive actions listed below are generally recommended in the case of kennels where bitches are bred regularly.

Husbandry

- Ensure that all puppies suck within the first hour or so of being born so that they get an adequate amount of colostrum. It is of note that colostrum is only absorbed from the intestines of puppies in the first few hours after birth. Colostrum substitutes are available if required.
- Provide a secluded whelping area that is adequately heated and properly ventilated (see Chapter Five).
- Check that the puppies are progressing satisfactorily by examining them closely, at least daily, and by weighing them regularly.
- In the case of large breeds, use a whelping box that will give protection against possible crushing (see Chapter Five).
- Adopt a sound disinfection policy. New, improved products are being continually developed. Ask your vet for his or her recommendation (see Chapter Four).
- Do not introduce new dogs or bitches into a breeding kennel without a period of isolation. It may be helpful to ask the owner of a selected sire to have preputial swabs taken and examined bacteriologically before mating, so that effective treatment can be given.
- Do not introduce bitches that are already pregnant into a breeding kennel.
- Instigate a regular worming policy for all stock. It is advisable to use the more recently introduced products that are active against migrating *Toxocara canis* (roundworm) larvae – your veterinary surgeon will advise.

Feeding

- Provide the bitch with an adequate quantity of a ready-prepared, complete, well-balanced diet from a reputable manufacturer. Pay particular attention to diet in the last third of pregnancy and during lactation. Make certain that the bitch has constant access to fresh, clean water.
- Do not over-supplement the diet with vitamins, especially vitamin A.
- Weigh the pups daily and give supplementary artificial feeding to weak puppies – those that are less than 75 per cent (three-quarters) of the normal birth weight for the breed – and those that are not gaining

weight steadily. Puppies should double their birth weight in seven to 10 days.

Medication

- Where fading litters have been shown to be due to a bacterial infection, seek veterinary advice before the bitch is mated again. A course of antibiotics given at mating, to cover the whelping period and possibly during pregnancy, may be recommended. It should be realised, however, that this may prevent the digestive organs of the puppies from working properly, and may, in fact, cause diarrhoea and failure to thrive. Never give antibiotics without precise veterinary advice on the dosage and the duration of administration.
- Ensure that breeding bitches are properly vaccinated and boosted against Infectious Canine Hepatitis. Recently a vaccine has been produced to protect against Canine Herpes virus infection. Ask your vet whether this may be useful in your case.

Retiring bitches from breeding

- Bitches that produce fading puppies, have dystocia, are bad mothers, or produce abnormally high numbers of puppies with significant congenital defects should not be used for breeding. Be prepared to ask for veterinary advice in this respect.

Record-keeping

- Good record-keeping is paramount to successful breeding. Ideally, an individual record card should be kept for each breeding bitch together with a separate mating/whelping register.

Comment

Kennel owners with a fading puppy problem should be prepared for a lengthy veterinary inspection of their premises and records, and a detailed examination of all their stock. In the majority of cases, bacterial swabs will have to be taken from the throats of all dogs, from the vulva of bitches, and from the sheath of any stud dogs. There may also be a need to examine blood samples (often a series) from all the bitches, puppies and dogs on the premises, and to carry out post-mortem examinations on puppies that have faded. It is obvious that such an investigation can be an expensive, time-consuming necessity. Thus, the rigorous application of the preventive measures noted above is well worthwhile, as considerable expense could be saved and the possible loss of a breeding line could be prevented.

THE NURSING BITCH

The energy requirements for the nursing (lactating) bitch are very much more demanding than pregnancy. All too often a bitch is seen to lose body condition rapidly when nursing her young, at the expense of her own body reserves.

This is because puppies will double their weight in about seven to 10 days. So, for example, a Beagle puppy weighing 10 oz (300 g) at birth will reach 1 lb 4 oz (600 g) eight days later. To provide for six puppies, the Beagle bitch will have to produce nearly a pint of milk (500 ml) a day at one week post-whelping. At four weeks after the birth, a bitch of this size will reach peak lactation, producing about two-and-a-half pints (1.5 litres) *each day* to meet the requirements of her litter, which by then could collectively weigh over half the bodyweight of their mother!

To meet these demands, and still maintain body condition, the bitch must steadily increase her food intake during the first four weeks of lactation. At the end of the first week, she will need about twice the normal adult maintenance levels; four weeks later, she should be eating nearly four times as much food than she ate before mating.

Even during early lactation, a bitch in these circumstances would be giving her puppies nearly ¼ lb (100 g) of actual protein (enough for a 50 lb/23 kg adult) via her milk each day. This protein needs to be made up in the diet by even more than this amount, as the efficiency of conversion into milk is less than 100 per cent.

The very high levels of all nutrients that any bitch with a fair-sized litter will need usually means that several meals will be required each day. The mother may even need to be fed more than once during the night, especially when the puppies' demands reach their peak. Feeding *ad libitum* is sometimes recommended. It obviously makes sense at this time to feed the more concentrated prepared foods that are available from a number of dog food manufacturers. These products, which are especially palatable, highly digestible and have a high calorific density, can be obtained from the better pet shops and pet superstores, as well as from many veterinary practices. Your vet will advise on the quantities needed if you are concerned.

If you have some leftover human food that contains good-quality protein, such as eggs, cheese, fish or the remains of a stew, this can be fed to the bitch but it should not make up more than 10 per cent of the bitch's total calorie intake.

Lactating bitches require a high fluid intake, and therefore a plentiful supply of fresh drinking water must always be made available.

Significant problems can arise if home-made diets are used, particularly at times of maximum demand. For example, if the extra energy needs are met with extra carbohydrate or fat, the mother may well satisfy her appetite before she has taken enough protein and she will use her own body reserves to make up the difference. Eventually she will fail to produce enough milk for her litter, and they will rapidly suffer from malnutrition if not given supplementary feeds.

After weaning is completed, the bitch's food intake should be adjusted to correct any of the changes in body weight or condition that have occurred during pregnancy and lactation. If feeding throughout has been correct, little adjustment should be necessary and the bitch can quickly return to her normal diet and feeding regime.

CARE OF PUPPIES: WEEKS 2-8

ACCOMMODATION
- **Outside kennels:** In the case of regular breeders, when puppies of the large breeds are between three to four weeks old, they may be moved to an outside purpose-built puppy kennel. It must be stressed, however, that adequate heating is still most important, and from the behaviour point of view, it is essential to ensure that the puppies are properly habituated and socialised (see Chapter Eight).
- **In the house:** If puppies are being raised in the house, they should be moved to more spacious quarters as they progress and start moving around the enclosed whelping box. As the puppies get older they will need to be accommodated in an improvised enclosed run or playpen, in a busier part of the home, usually the kitchen. This serves the purpose of allowing the puppies to see and hear everything that is going on in the household, and, at the same time, keeping them out of harm's way. The puppies will also have the opportunity to get used to being handled more often. Ideally, the litter should be raised in a corner of the kitchen in an enclosed area containing a warm bed. Bedding will need to be changed as soon as it is soiled, so a good supply of easily laundered bedding is essential. Polyester fleece is especially comfortable for the puppies, as the surface is always warm and dry. It has the added advantage that it gives the young puppies something to grip when they move around the whelping box. The floor of the enclosure should be covered in newspaper to encourage the young puppies to leave the bed and consequently learn not to soil it. Generally, dogs and even young puppies will instinctively not soil the nest – so this is the very first step in house-training the puppies.

FEEDING

The bitch's milk should remain as the major source of food until the puppies are at least three weeks old. They should start to take an interest in solid food as they begin to explore their surroundings. Usually at around this age, they will start to eat their mother's food and can be allowed free access to it, provided it is of good quality. Puppies can be reared very successfully on soft, highly nutritious and palatable proprietary puppy diets. Many breeders, however, start off more cautiously by giving scraped beef, porridge or cereal with a little milk and scrambled eggs before introducing ready-prepared puppy food. Some bitches will, at this stage, regurgitate a quantity of their own food for their puppies to eat. This is quite natural and is not a cause for concern; such behaviour does not usually go on for more than a few days.

It is unwise to raise puppies exclusively on home-made diets as they grow bigger because nutritional deficiencies can easily result. However, proprietary foods can be supplemented with scrambled eggs, fish, milk and cereals if these foods are available, and if it is considered appropriate. This will provide some variety and accustom the puppy to the taste of different foods, which could well be advantageous later in the puppy's life. These foods should only be given in small quantities and, as mentioned previously, make up no more than 10 per cent of the total ration so that the balance of the prepared food is not adversely affected.

The bitch should be separated from her puppies more frequently, and for progressively long periods of time, during weaning. This will allow her milk supply to dry up, and will enable the puppies to adapt gradually to their new source of food. There are no hard-and-fast rules in this respect, you will need to be guided by common sense, the bitch's demeanour and the contentment of the puppies.

Puppies should be offered food in shallow bowls, and they should be carefully supervised to ensure that they do not urinate or defecate in the containers. Some puppies may need to be encouraged to eat solid food by letting them lick some off your fingers; most will quickly learn to eat from a bowl. As the puppies grow older they can be fed away from their mother – it is best to aim for independence at six weeks of age. By the time they are ready to be homed, they should be eating four substantial meals a day.

FUNDAMENTAL CONSIDERATIONS

Puppies can be reared very satisfactorily on a wide variety of diets. However, the factors noted below are extremely important:
• First, to provide for growth, puppies need larger amounts of food, relative to their weight, than fully-grown adults. (See Figure 15.)

- Secondly, puppies have small stomachs, relative to the quantity of food they need. Thus, they need to be fed several times a day. Up to 12 weeks of age they will require four meals daily, spread evenly throughout the day from early morning until late at night. The number of feeds given daily can be reduced gradually to two by six to nine months of age. (See Table 4.)
- A highly digestible, concentrated, very palatable, balanced diet is required for growth. Good-quality protein is particularly important.
- Any changes in diet must be introduced gradually to avoid possible digestive upsets.
- When using ready-prepared diets, the feeding instructions should be read carefully and followed precisely.
- If you have any concerns, help can be obtained from the staff at your veterinary surgery, or possibly from an experienced dog breeder, staff at a good pet shop or pet superstore, or from a food manufaccturer.

FIGURE 15: FEEDING REQUIREMENTS DURING GROWTH (TAKEN FROM THE WALTAM BOOK OF COMPANION ANIMAL NUTRITION BY I. BURGER, 1995)

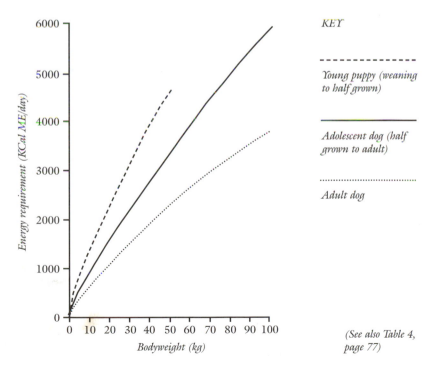

KEY

Young puppy (weaning to half grown)

Adolescent dog (half grown to adult)

Adult dog

(See also Table 4, page 77)

PREVENTIVE MEDICINE

When puppies are six weeks of age, a veterinary surgeon should be consulted about the programme of routine vaccinations for any you are keeping for yourself and for bespoke puppies in accordance with the new owner's wishes. By this stage, you should already have wormed the puppies two or possibly three times, to eliminate the roundworm *Toxocara canis* (see Chapter Seven).

FEEDING ORPHAN AND PREMATURE PUPPIES

The best way to feed orphaned puppies is to use a foster bitch, but that is rarely possible, as it requires another bitch, with a small litter, or possibly one whose puppies are just being weaned. Sometimes a bitch lactating as a result of false pregnancy can be used to raise puppies, and such bitches often make very good foster mothers.

The alternative is to supply a substitute milk. However, you should be aware that handrearing is a major undertaking involving not only the feeding of puppies, but also, in very young puppies, the need to stimulate urination and defecation and to keep them clean.

Proprietary bitch replacement milks are the most satisfactory substitutes for bitch's milk, and should be fed according to the directions given. Cow's or goat's milk should not be fed alone, as both contain too little protein, fat, calcium and energy, and are not sufficiently concentrated. Evaporated and condensed milks are not suitable, as they contain too much lactose, which can cause severe diarrhoea in young puppies, resulting in further complications, such as dehydration.

Looking after motherless puppies is a very demanding undertaking, requiring considerable commitment in time and patience – for example, very young puppies need feeding at least every four hours, day and night. For the novice, the guidance of a veterinary surgeon or experienced breeder is essential; they will be able to advise precisely how to use a feeding bottle with a teat, tube or a syringe to give the puppies the milk substitute, with minimum risk of the fluid being inhaled into the lungs.

CARE OF PUPPIES: AFTER 8 WEEKS

Hopefully, by this time, all the puppies, with the possible exception of any that you are keeping for yourself, will be bespoke. You will, of course, have spent time questioning prospective owners about their lifestyle and have asked the question: "Why do you want to have a dog and one of my puppies particularly?" Do be prepared to ask penetrating questions, and, if you are not happy, be strong enough to say so. In this way you will have peace of mind, knowing that you have done your very best by the puppies you have raised.

Conscientious breeders will want to see that the puppies they have raised have a good start in life with the real expectation of being 'ideal dogs'. Some of the more important matters to which attention should be given are noted below. However, it is not within the scope of this book to go into detail, thus we do recommend that you suggest to new puppy owners that they purchase a copy of *Puppylopaedia*, which is the companion volume to this book. That will provide a readily accessible source of information, which they can refer to at their leisure. This is helpful because much of the advice you give when the owners collect the puppy will be forgotten in the excitement of the moment.

FEEDING

You should tell the purchasers of your puppies exactly how you have been feeding the puppies, giving details of the quantities, frequency and products used. It is most important that they do not make any major changes early on, and any modifications to the diet that are made later must be done gradually to avoid digestive upsets.

It is usual to recommend the following feeding routine:

TABLE 4: FREQUENCY OF FEEDING FOR PUPPIES

Age of dog/puppy	Number of meals per day
8-12 weeks	4
3-6 months	3
6-9 months	2
9 months +	1 or 2 as convenient

PREVENTIVE MEDICINE

It is important that you give new owners full details of what actions you have taken with regard to vaccination, worming and the control of ectoparasites.

BEHAVIOUR

Puppy owners will be most appreciative if you can tell them how, and what, you have achieved in respect of house-training and other behaviour modification techniques you have employed (see Chapter Eight).

EQUIPMENT

Be prepared to give puppy owners advice about what equipment you consider best, particularly regarding bedding, collars, leads, feeding and drinking bowls, and grooming tools.

DOG IDENTIFICATION

Advise new owners of the law relating to dog identification (see below).

A licence to own a dog in the UK is no longer needed. However, all dog owners are still legally required to ensure that their dog wears a collar with a tag at all times when he is away from his own property. That necessity apart, it makes sense to identify all brood bitches and stud dogs by one of the more permanent methods that are currently available. This will help to ensure that they can be recognised and returned should they become lost or are stolen.

DOG TAGS

As noted above, it is mandatory for all dogs to wear a tag (usually an engraved metal disc) attached to their collars, showing clearly the owner's name, address, telephone number and possibly the dog's name. Owners are responsible for ensuring that the lettering on the tag does not become blurred, that it can be easily read, and that the information is up to date.

TATTOOING

Tattooing is a proven, permanent method of identification which is recognised by the Companion Animal Welfare Council (CAWC) as being acceptable. The dog is marked with indelible ink with a seven-figure number on either the ear flap or, less commonly, the inside of the thigh. Puppies can be tattooed before they leave the nest, usually when they are six to eight weeks of age. The procedure is relatively quickly accomplished, but the service of a skilled tattooist is needed, which can be expensive. The tattoo mark is recorded by a central body, which may be contacted, if a stray is found, to establish the dog's identity and locate the owner.

The main disadvantages of tattooing are: that it is not an acceptable method of identification for the Pet Travel Scheme (PETS), and the ink may fade over time, necessitating further tattooing. However, it does have the advantage of being a quick and visible method of identification, which can discourage theft.

When exporting dogs to some countries, such as Canada, a tattoo is a necessary requirement.

MICRO-CHIPPING

The 'state of the art' identity marker is undoubtedly the implanted identity 'chip'; a small bar-coded pellet that is implanted between the shoulder blades at the base of the dog's neck. The implant can be put in place when the puppies are just a few weeks old; they last for life, cannot be altered and can easily be 'read' by a transponder (similar to the instrument used to read bar codes in supermarket checkouts). Most major rescue homes have these readers, as do the police, local authorities and most veterinary surgeries. Information relating to the dog and his owner can be obtained from a central data-base once the number encoded on the chip has been identified.

Chipping is not difficult and can, in fact, be carried out by any trained person – a veterinary qualification is not required. Properly done, the procedure is painless for the dog, as the actual chip is no larger than a grain of rice. Ideally, the micro-chip should be checked regularly every time the dog is taken to a veterinary surgery to ensure that it is still working and has not 'migrated' to another site, possibly the shoulder or the elbow. In this connection, it is worth noting that dogs should always be implanted when standing, not when lying on their sides. The more modern micro-chips are speccially designed to help prevent migration from the site of implantation.

Micro-chipping has become the most popular method of permanently identifying dogs, and is recognised by the British Small Animal Veterinary Association as being safe and reliable. The Kennel Club runs Petlog (see Appendix 4), which is the largest pet identification and reunification scheme in the UK for dogs who have been micro-chipped.

To qualify for the Pet Travel Scheme (PETS), dogs *must* be implanted with a micro-chip so that they can be properly identified. Full detail about the regulations with regard to taking dogs overseas, and for dogs entering or re-entering the UK, can be obtained from PETS/DEFRA (see Useful Contacts, Appendix 4).

Finally, micro-chipping is really a necessity in breeding kennels so that breeding bitches and stud dogs can be positively identified, and to provide definitive information when samples are submitted for health and genetic testing.

It is probably sensible if you own a registered pedigree bitch to ask your vet to implant your dog with a micro-chip that is part of the Kennel Club's PetLog scheme. Your details will be sent to PetLog for registration, and they will remain on the database free of charge for the lifetime of your pet. If your pet strays or is stolen and is subsequently found, you can be traced by the police, veterinary surgeons or animal welfare organisation who scans your pet and reads the micro-chip number. The Petlog reunification service even works if your pet is lost when you are travelling in Europe! (See Appendix 4.)

INSURANCE
It can be helpful to give new owners details of the insurance company you use, to help them decide what policies are available and to choose one for themselves. (See also notes below.)

All dog owners should have public liability insurance, which will indemnify them in the case of accidents to the general public or damage to other people's property. It is indeed possible that third-party insurance will become a legal requirement for dog owners in the UK in the future. Household insurance policies sometimes provide cover for the owner but not the dog; the animal is therefore only covered when it is in the care and control of the insured householder or his/her family.

Dog owners can, if they wish, cover the cost of veterinary attention, in the case of accident or illness. In this connection, it should be noted that although insurance premiums have increased lately, the cover provided is still good value. The cost of veterinary treatment has risen dramatically recently, as diagnostic aids have become more complex and are employed more often, and drugs and equipment are also much more expensive. Furthermore, cases are much more frequently referred to consultants, with the result that treatment can become considerably more costly.

Generally, standard insurance policies cover veterinary fees for illness and accident (up to £5,000 for each incident), early death, death through illness, boarding kennel fees, holiday cancellation, overseas travel, theft, straying, third-party cover and even behaviour and bereavement counselling. They do not usually cover preventive vaccination, elective neutering, Caesarean section, death of a bitch prenatally, or the death of newborn puppies.

It is a good idea to check with the insurer to establish whether any of these risks are covered and, if not, the likely cost of doing so. It is also sensible for prospective breeders to contact the major insurance companies to identify whether any of their standard policies will provide the particular cover needed. At least one company will insure bitch owners for veterinary fees that may be incurred during pregnancy and whelping, and often policies can be 'tailor-made' to meet specific requirements, such as breeding risks. However, do take care when selecting a company to compare like with like and also to check the excess and exclusion clauses.

For regular breeders, insurance is available that will cover puppies when they go to their new homes. This insurance generally starts the moment the new owner collects the puppy from the breeder, and is seen as a positive service offered by the breeder. The breeder of the puppy gives details of the new owner to the insurance company, issues a cover note for the puppy, stating that it shows no signs of disease, and the puppy is then fully covered for most risks for the next six weeks. During that time, the insurance company will usually contact the new owner, inviting them to continue the cover for the following years. Similar cover is offered by the Kennel Club when puppies are registered with the club (see Appendix 2). In this context, it should be noted that the rules governing the recommendation of specific insurance companies are continually changing. Therefore, advice should be obtained by the breeder from their insurance company before a recommendation is given to anyone.

VETERINARY ADVICE
Provide details of the veterinary surgery you have attended to all the puppy purchasers if the new owners are living in your area.

EXERCISE
Do let new puppy owners know what the exercise requirement of their puppy will be as it grows up. Be prepared to share your experience in this respect.

KENNEL CLUB REGISTRATION
In the case of pedigree puppies, you will need to pass on all the necessary documents and information concerning Kennel Club registration (see Appendix 2).

> *Finally, while giving the information noted above, take the opportunity to ensure that you are happy that the puppy you have raised is going to a good home where it will be properly looked after. If you are unhappy or have any major doubts, it is better to withdraw at this stage than to regret it later.*

CHAPTER 7

PREVENTIVE MEDICINE

1. Health checks for bitches
2. Gynaecological records
3. Recognising illness in dogs
4. Endoparasite infectons
5. Ectoparasite infections
6. Inherited diseases and conditions

As the old proverb states: *prevention is better than cure*. Taking steps to ensure that your bitch is protected against common ailments and diseases can save a great deal of heartache, time and money.

HEALTH CHECKS FOR BITCHES

BROOD BITCHES
Although the health checks described below are relevant to all bitches throughout their lives, it is particularly important that they are carried out meticulously during the months preceding a planned mating. The examinations noted are best carried out during routine grooming.

- **Eyes:** should be checked *daily* for inflammatory changes, tear staining or excessive or abnormally coloured discharge.
- **Ears:** should be checked on a *weekly* basis to ensure that no discharge or obnoxious odour is coming from the ear canal.
- **Nails:** need checking *monthly* for length and splitting, and the nail beds should be observed for any signs of excessive inflammation.
- **Teeth and mouth:** should also be checked *monthly* for dental decay,

the accumulation of tartar and inflammation of the gums.
- **Skin:** should be inspected at least on a *weekly* basis for inflammation, abrasions, hair loss, wounds and the presence of ectoparasites.
- **Faeces:** note as far as possible, *daily*, any deviations from the norm in respect of colour, frequency and consistency. If any changes are seen, check the dog for other signs of illness, and think back with the objective of identifying whether the problem could be linked to a change in diet or something that may have been scavenged.

As well as the examinations noted above, some special checks should be carried out by all bitch owners at least monthly, and, ideally, more frequently when bitches are due in season. These checks are particularly important in the case of regular breeders and for pet owners who want to breed from their bitch, or need to, under a breeding terms agreement.
- **Urination:** Note the frequency and, if possible, the colour of urine passed. More frequent 'squatting' may indicate that your bitch is about to come on heat or an impending urino-genital tract infection.
- **Thirst:** Check how much water is being drunk. Excessive thirst may indicate impending pyometra, diabetes or a urinary tract infection.
- **Behaviour:** Look for changes in behaviour, such as more frequent urination and territory marking, which may indicate that your bitch is about to come on heat, have a false pregnancy or an impending illness.
- **Vulva:** Look for abnormal swelling, wounds, signs of excessive licking or a discharge. Pay particular attention at the time the bitch is on heat and for the following two to three months.
- **Mammary glands:** Look for the presence of milk by gently squeezing the teats. Feel all the mammary glands for tumours and record their size. It is particularly important to carry out this examination when the bitch is on heat and weekly in the subsequent two to three months.
- **Skin/coat:** Look for thickened skin or baldness, particularly on the elbows, flanks and hocks. Loss of hair, especially on the flanks, is often associated with some hormonal deficiencies, especially in short-coated breeds like Dobermanns. If these changes are seen, seek veterinary advice before mating, since fertility may be affected.
- **Post-whelping:** Special diligence is needed in the weeks post-whelping in checking the mammary glands and the appearance and odour of any remaining vaginal discharge. Such observations should be carried out daily at least until weaning starts, and then twice weekly until the puppies are separated from the bitch. If any abnormalities are discovered, their significance and the need for medication should be discussed with a veterinary surgeon.

GYNAECOLOGICAL RECORDS

Keeping good records is fundamental to good dog breeding practice, and this is particularly so in the case of regular breeders. The tables below are examples of how this need can be satisfied quite easily. They are intended simply for guidance and can, of course, be modified to meet any specific circumstance.

TABLE 5: GYNAECOLOGICAL RECORDS/BREEDING NOTES

BREEDING NOTES		Heat Number					
Event/Date		1	2	3	4	5	6
Heat	Start						
	End						
False pregnancy	Start						
	End						
Mating dates	First						
	Second						
Whelping	Start date/time						
	End date/time						
No. pups (male/female)	Born						
	Reared						

MEDICAL NOTES			
Condition	Date	Medication/surgery	Comments/result

GENERAL NOTES

RECOGNISING ILLNESS IN DOGS

Usually in books of this nature, the signs shown by dogs suffering from the main diseases that affect them are given in detail. This approach is doubtless of interest, and, in some respects, instructive; indeed we adopted this format ourselves in *Doglopaedia*. Some problems with following this route are: first, that in the case of many common diseases, the signs are very much the same; they are not specific. Secondly, not all affected dogs show all the signs noted. This means that diagnosis can be extremely difficult for owners in many cases, making it necessary and sensible to seek the help of an experienced veterinary surgeon, who may well need to carry out laboratory tests to confirm a tentative diagnosis. Left on their own, owners may well jump to a wrong conclusion and this could lead to delayed or ineffective treatment.

In view of the difficulties noted above, we decided, when planning this book, to depart from the traditional approach and give readers guidance simply on how to identify when a pet is just off colour, when it has a mild illness, or when it is showing signs of a more serious disease or condition. Hopefully, this will lead to the earlier recognition of significant illness, more prompt treatment and, thus, less suffering and pain. Our objective then, is to help owners to identify and describe accurately the signs of illness and pain in their pet, to build up a meaningful 'history' of the problem, and to know if, and when, veterinary advice should be sought. An accurate account of the pet's illness will go a long way to ensuring a quicker, more definitive diagnosis. This, in turn, will lead to the administration of the most appropriate medication more promptly, reducing the duration of the illness and, incidentally, the cost of treatment.

WHAT TO LOOK FOR

EARLY SIGNS
- **Changed behaviour:** By and large, dogs are creatures of habit, so any variation from a dog's normal behaviour that is not provoked by a notable change in circumstances may well indicate that a dog is generally unwell.
- **Inappetence (refusal to eat):** Refusal to eat is often the first sign of illness, but is only of real significance if persistent. Many perfectly healthy dogs will refuse to eat the occasional meal or two.
- **Raised temperature:** Dogs with raised temperatures will seek a cooler place to lie, they will pant and may feel hot to the touch. We do *not* recommend that owners, with the possible exception of regular

breeders who have been instructed by their veterinary surgeon, make any attempt to take a dog's temperature with a mercury thermometer. Such instruments can only too easily become broken in the dog's anus. Digital thermometers are available and can be used, since they are more robust. However, it is worthy of note that the actual recorded temperature needs skilled interpretation. Anxious dogs often show a much higher temperature than normal.

- **General weakness and lethargy:** If not associated with hot weather or excessive exercise, weakness and lethargy could be an indication of some systemic disease and warrants an early veterinary investigation if the signs persist for more than two to three days.
- **Pain:** Pain will be evidenced by crying (unprovoked vocalisation), cringing and possibly aggression. Dogs in pain will constantly turn and glance at the source of the pain, and possibly bite at the affected area. Dogs in pain will be reluctant to leave their beds and will resent the site of the pain being touched.

If any of the signs noted above persist for more than two to three days, consider seeking veterinary assistance.

MORE SPECIFIC SIGNS
- **Lameness, a staggering gait or incoordination:** Lameness may occur through pain, or it may be mechanical (stiffness in a joint, for example). Lameness and change in gait, or incoordination, may stem from the legs or possibly the dog's back. Generally speaking, if lameness is due to pain in the foot, the leg will be carried; if the site of the pain is higher up the leg, the dog will limp. Lameness associated with significant pain calls for prompt veterinary treatment. In cases of mild lameness without pain, veterinary attention should be sought at your earliest convenience. Acute lameness, which could have been caused by an accident, obviously calls for prompt veterinary assistance.
- **Vomiting:** Occasional vomiting (perhaps after a dog has eaten grass) is of no importance. However, prolonged or persistent vomiting is significant and veterinary help should be obtained without delay. If the vomit contains blood, this is generally serious and represents an emergency; consult your vet promptly.
- **Drinking excessively:** Always pay attention to the amount of water your dog drinks daily so that you will be able to detect any increase in thirst without delay. Obviously, dogs will drink more in hot conditions, or if their food has contained larger amounts of salt than

is normally the case. That apart, excessive drinking is a significant sign and may indicate kidney disease or diabetes, or, in bitches, possibly pyometra. Consult your vet promptly if your bitch starts to drink large quantities of water soon after she has been on heat. In other cases, seek veterinary help if excessive drinking continues for more than three or four days.

- **Eye discharge:** A slight or clear discharge from the eyes is quite normal, but seek veterinary advice promptly if the discharge is profuse or contains pus. If you suspect the discharge is associated with a wound to the surface of the eye, possibly after fighting with a cat or being knocked by the end of a lead, get veterinary help without delay.

- **Head-shaking and scratching the ears:** This can be an early sign of ear disease (ear canker). If a discharge is coming from the ears and/or there are signs of inflammation or an unpleasant smell, make an early appointment to see your vet. If head shaking and ear scratching occurs suddenly, or if the dog holds his head on one side (particularly if you have recently been in fields with long grass), and he is obviously distressed, you should seek veterinary help urgently. The dog may well have a grass seed in his ear that needs prompt removal. Never poke inside a dog's ear or try to treat ear problems with human medication. Ear canker (otitis externa) has a number of different causes, and specific treatment is needed.

- **Abnormal breathing:** Unless more rapid or difficult breathing is associated simply with a high ambient temperature, strenuous exercise or obvious nervousness, these signs should be regarded as an emergency. This is because such breathing abnormalities can be associated with a number of serious conditions, such as an obstructed airway or heart disease. Thus, it is sensible to seek veterinary assistance without delay.

- **Diarrhoea:** The more frequent passage of liquid faeces (diarrhoea) is most commonly caused by digestive upsets. If you think this is the problem, withhold food for 12 hours but ensure that drinking water is freely available. When food is reinstated, give scrambled eggs and white fish, together with plain boiled rice, in small quantities for a day or two, and then gradually return to the dog's normal diet. If the diarrhoea persists or, importantly, if the faeces contain blood, seek veterinary attention without delay.

- **Problems with passing urine:** Withholding urine may be voluntary, especially in bitches – for example when confined to a car or not having access to the outside. In this case, the cure is obvious and there is no cause for alarm. In other situations, failing to pass urine or straining to pass urine is always a serious emergency and must never be neglected for more than 24 hours. Bitches may show blood in their urine when on heat or after whelping, but if this happens at any other time, it is a serious sign and a veterinary surgeon should be consulted as soon as possible.

- **Discharge from the penis or vulva:** It is normal for bitches and dogs to clean their genitalia by licking – a small amount of discharge is no cause for concern. However, if the discharge is excessive or has an obnoxious smell then veterinary help should be sought within two to three days. Bitches suffering from 'open' pyometra may pass copious amounts of bloodstained, foul-smelling discharge from the vulva. If this is suspected (shortly after the bitch has been on heat), veterinary attention is needed without any delay whatsoever.

- **Nasal discharge:** It is normal for dogs to have a cool, moist nose, but, in contrast, a warm, dry nose is not necessarily an indication that a dog is unwell. A small drop of watery mucus coming from the nostrils is quite normal, and this should simply be removed gently with a piece of damp cotton wool when the dog is groomed. However, if the discharge becomes thick or contains pus or blood, seek veterinary assistance at once. There may be an injury to the nose, something may have become stuck in the nostril, or it may be an early sign of a major respiratory infection.

- **Coughing:** An occasional cough is nothing to be alarmed about, especially when it occurs after exuberant play or over-enthusiastic barking. However, persistent coughing – especially if phlegm is coughed up – could indicate a lung or heart problem and it is wise to seek veterinary attention without too much delay. Coughing is, of course, a regular sign in dogs suffering from Canine Distemper (although that disease is very rare these days) or Kennel Cough. In the latter case, there is usually a history of the dog being kennelled recently, or having been in close contact with other coughing dogs. If Kennel Cough is suspected, seek prompt veterinary assistance. Early treatment will mean a quicker recovery and less expense. In older dogs, persistent non-productive coughing, especially after exercise, is often a sign associated with heart disease.

- **Difficulty eating:** In older dogs this sign is often associated with tooth decay or gum disease. In younger dogs it can be associated with a foreign body lodged in the mouth (most commonly a piece of bone or a stick). If the problem persists, or the dog shows signs of pain and distress, as evidenced by continual pawing at the mouth, a prompt veterinary consultation is called for.

- **Fits, convulsions or collapse:** If a dog shows any of these signs, veterinary help must be sought as an emergency.
- **Lumps or swellings:** Lumps or swellings should be investigated by a veterinary surgeon if they do not disappear within a few days or are accompanied by a raised temperature. It always makes sense to monitor the size of any swellings by comparing them with a nut, fruit or vegetable; if they are increasing significantly in size, or appear to be troubling the dog, consult your vet.

The list given above is, of course, not exhaustive. If you are particularly worried about an unusual sign shown by your dog, it is always wise to consult your veterinary surgeon without too much delay – if only to save you worrying and to give you peace of mind. Don't be put off because you think your vet may be too busy to be concerned with something that may appear of only questionable significance. It is better to be safe than sorry.

VACCINATION
Five serious diseases threaten dogs throughout their lives:
- **Canine Distemper:** A viral infection that causes dogs to have runny eyes, diarrhoea, a discharge from the nose and a severe cough. These signs are often followed by the hardening of the foot pads and nervous signs, including fits, which frequently prove fatal.
- **Infectious Canine Hepatitis:** A extremely contagious viral disease, which can be fatal within as little as 24 hours, allowing no time for effective treatment. It can also cause liver and kidney damage in the long-term and may affect the eyes (Blue Eye).
- **Canine Parvovirus Infection:** A very serious disease that emerged in the 1970s, which can cause heart problems and pneumonia in young puppies, and, in older puppies and adults, severe vomiting and diarrhoea (often containing large amounts of blood). The disease may be rapidly fatal in young puppies and also in older dogs if treatment is delayed.
- **Leptospirosis:** The two forms of leptospirosis are caused by bacteria called leptospires. Affected dogs run a high temperature, vomit severely and often become jaundiced. Those dogs that do not die may suffer from chronic liver or kidney damage later in life. These infections can affect people.
- **Kennel Cough:** An irritating disease complex that can be caused by a number of infectious agents, including the bacterium *Bordetella bronchiseptica* and a number of viruses, particularly Canine

Parainfluenza virus, acting alone or in combination. This disease, although only rarely fatal, often calls for expensive, protracted treatment. Puppies and older dogs are particularly vulnerable. Kennel Cough is not only picked up in kennels: any dog-to-dog contact (for example, at dog shows) can lead to a susceptible animal becoming infected.

Fortunately, effective vaccines are available to protect dogs against all the infectious diseases noted above. Their use can give pet owners and dog breeders peace of mind and save dogs from suffering and perhaps dying prematurely. Veterinary advice is required so that the most cost-effective vaccination programme can be selected in any specific situation.

Apart from the diseases mentioned above, it has recently become possible to vaccinate dogs against Canine Herpes virus infection and Canine Corono virus infection. The former virus is one of the causes of death in young puppies (fading puppies) and may be involved as a cause of Kennel Cough, and the latter virus is now considered to be responsible for a higher frequency of canine enteritis than previously realised.

BROOD BITCHES

All bitches used for breeding purposes should be comprehensively protected against all the infections described earlier by primary and booster vaccination. Normally, it is best to complete a vaccination course early in life. If that has not been the case, a full vaccination regime should be completed at least a month or two before bitches are mated (rather than during pregnancy). If there are any doubts about this matter, veterinary advice should be sought. Regular breeders should also ensure that any stud dogs they use have undergone a complete primary vaccination programme and have also been given regular boosters.

PUPPIES

Puppies have an immune system of their own at birth, but it does not become fully active until they are a few weeks old. Thus, nature has arranged for them to acquire some protective antibodies from their mother (so-called maternally derived passive antibodies). To reduce the risk of disease early in life, such passive antibodies are passed to puppies while they are in the womb and through the colostrum or first milk. Most of this passive protection comes from the latter source. Since antibodies in the colostrum can only be absorbed by puppies for the first day or so of their lives, it is obvious that pups should be encouraged to suck vigorously as soon as possible after being born. The antibodies passed to puppies in this way will give protection against all the diseases to which the mother has been exposed or been vaccinated against.

On average, the level of antibodies in the puppy's blood is approximately 77 per cent of that in its mother's blood. Because maternally derived antibody has been passively acquired, it wanes quite quickly – the quantity in the blood is halved every seven to eight days. Obviously, the duration of this passive protection in an individual puppy is dependant on the mother's own level of protection. These facts highlight the important role that needs to be played by breeders, namely to ensure that breeding bitches are properly vaccinated, and that puppies are encouraged to suck effectively in the first few hours of their lives.

A significant, complicating factor is that maternally derived antibodies not only protect against disease but also prevent a proper response to vaccination. Because the duration of maternally derived antibodies is determined by the level of the mother's immunity and the amount of colostrum ingested, the earliest age at which puppies will respond effectively to vaccination will vary considerably between litters, and, to some extent, even between individuals within a litter. Much research has gone into devising vaccination regimes that will leave puppies exposed to the risk of infection for the shortest possible period of time. In other words, to reduce the so-called 'immunity gap'.

More recently still, vaccines have been developed that are capable of stimulating immunity 'in the face of' maternally derived antibody. This means that puppies can now be vaccinated at six weeks of age in some situations – a great advantage in respect of the need for early habituation and socialisation. Now that the pressing need for early socialisation has been highlighted (see Chapter Eight) it is particularly helpful if breeders offer to puppy purchasers the possibility of having their puppy vaccinated *before they are homed*. The cost of providing this service can, of course, be included in the cost of the puppy, or at least discussed with the new owner.

Puppy vaccination is obviously a complex matter and, thus, there is the need to rely on veterinary advice as to what is the best routine to adopt in your particular case, and which specific vaccine is most appropriate to your needs.

The levels of *active* antibodies stimulated by vaccination wane much more slowly than is the case with passively acquired antibodies. Nevertheless, regular booster doses of vaccine are required – either annually or every other year – to maintain immunity. Your veterinary surgeon is the best person to guide you in this respect; do remember to tell him or her of any breeding plans you may have.

> *Note: The need for booster doses of vaccine and their frequency is a matter of some debate and controversy at this time. Do be guided by your veterinary surgeon, who will have had access to the latest scientific information on this matter. In our opinion, for peace of mind, it makes sense not to reduce by too much the frequency of repeat vaccinations. Also, no one wants the return of Canine Distemper or Canine Parvovirus infections with all the suffering that these diseases can cause. It is as well to remember that vaccination largely eliminated these diseases, and it is important not to become complacent and lower our guard.*

ENDOPARASITE INFECTIONS

Endoparasites are those that live inside the body. A number of endoparasite infections are of importance in bitches generally, and they are of particular significance in breeding stock, whether they are pet bitches or owned by regular breeders. The information given here is of particular relevance to owners of breeding kennels, since it is essential to keep these infections under control – *prevention* is paramount.

WORMS COMMONLY SEEN IN THE UK

A great variety of worms can infect dogs in the UK, but two are particularly common and important in all breeds. They are:
• The roundworm – *Toxocara canis*
• The tapeworm – *Dipylidium caninum*

Worm tablets can be purchased from either a chemist or pet shop, but it is necessary to know the type of worm infecting a dog in order to buy the correct remedy. Sometimes, in heavy roundworm infections, live worms are vomited, and tapeworm segments may be seen around the anus in dogs infected with *Diplydium caninum*. However, diagnosis is often difficult, as neither of these worms cause specific signs. Tapeworms rarely cause noticeable clinical signs, apart from possibly anal irritation and digestive disturbances, but roundworm infections may be associated with poor growth, diarrhoea, constipation, abdominal pain, possibly a pot-bellied appearance, and a decreased or increased appetite. Of course, all these signs can also be associated with other diseases and, thus, it makes sense to consult your vet if you are concerned. A sample of your dog's motions (faeces) will need to be examined to find out what eggs are present in order to prescribe the right treatment.

In the case of the tapeworm *D. caninum* infection, your vet will also advise you how to control fleas, and in respect of *T. canis* infection, you will be advised particularly about the need to use a product that is effective against migrating larvae as well as the adult worms.

The elimination of the roundworm *Toxocara canis* is important because this parasite can cause problems in people. Such cases are highlighted in the press, and are often exaggerated by the anti-dog lobby. If everyone who owns a dog follows the simple advice given below, the already low risk of damage to sight, which may be associated with this infection in children, could be reduced still further and possibly even eliminated.

TOXOCARA CANIS: ESSENTIAL FACTS
- *Toxocara canis* is a round white worm three to six inches in length.
- Currently, virtually all puppies are born infected to bitches that have not been wormed during pregnancy. Puppies will have adult worms in their intestines capable of laying eggs by the time they are 21 to 30 days old.
- Puppies under three months old can be infected by worm eggs on grass or plants in the garden, or on the bitch's coat. These hatch in the puppy's stomach, moving through the body and back to the intestine where they become adult. Puppies can also be infected by immature worms in their mother's milk.
- In puppies over three months of age, the larvae make only a limited migration and lie dormant in the body tissues, particularly in the muscles, the diaphragm and kidneys.
- When bitches become pregnant, the larvae lying dormant are stimulated to migrate again. They reach the womb and the mammary glands, infecting the puppies and completing the cycle.
- Around 30 to 40 per cent of puppies less than three months of age have adult worms in their intestines, which are able to pass eggs into the environment.
- Eggs in freshly voided faeces are not infective to dogs or people. Eggs take two to three weeks to become infective.

DIPYLIDIUM CANINUM: ESSENTIAL FACTS
- This worm, which lives in the small intestines of a dog, is a flat, segmented worm that can measure up to 20 inches (50 cm) in length.
- It is unusual to see a complete tapeworm shed in the faeces of infected dogs, but the individual segments, loaded with ripe eggs, are frequently seen emerging from the anus or attached to the hair under the tail. They look like grains of rice or cucumber seeds. These

segments are irritant and may cause the dog to scoot along the ground on his bottom.

- Fleas are a necessary part of the life cycle of *D. caninium*. Immature flea larvae swallow the worm eggs shed by dogs and these mature into an intermediate larval stage of the worm, called a metacestode, as the flea larvae develops into an adult flea.
- When a dog kills and eats a flea containing metacestodes, these worm larvae are released in the dog's intestine and develop into adult worms.
- Prevention of infection with this tapeworm requires maintaining a regular campaign against fleas on the dog and around the home.

PREVENTING *TOXOCARA CANIS* INFECTION IN PEOPLE

PUPPIES

- Puppies should be wormed regularly as directed by a veterinary surgeon. This usually means dosing puppies for three consecutive days at two and five weeks of age, and again before leaving for their new home. Treatment may also be required at 12 weeks of age. Thereafter, the frequency of treatment can be reduced unless the puppies remain in kennels where re-infection can occur only too readily. A newer product is available that is administered monthly from two weeks of age. Your vet will advise you on the use of any newly developed products and the course of action that is most relevant in your case.
- Puppies should ideally be trained to defecate in a specific fenced-off area in the garden before they are taken for walks.
- Faeces from dogs less than six months old must be picked up promptly because they may be harbouring adult worms in their intestines. Such faeces should be buried deeply or flushed down the toilet.
- Because they may be harbouring adult worms in their intestines capable of shedding eggs, dogs under six months of age should not be exercised in public places where children play or where families picnic.

ADULT BITCHES

- Speak to your vet about controlling heat in your bitch if you decide not to breed from her, or when she is retired. Bitches that do not come in heat, are, like dogs, much less likely to pass on infection. This is because, in entire bitches, dormant larval forms can be stimulated to start migrating again during pregnancy and false pregnancy, with the result that the adult worms are re-established in the intestine. In entire bitches, worming during false pregnancy has been recommended.

- All bitches should be wormed during pregnancy with a product that is effective against migrating larvae. The usually adopted regime is to treat pregnant bitches daily from day 40 of pregnancy through to two days post-whelping.

Note: Breeders, whether they be occasional or regular, have an important role to fulfil in respect of worm infections generally, and particularly concerning <u>Toxocara canis,</u> in ensuring that the information given above is passed on to new puppy owners.

A recent trial has shown that there may be a link between <u>T. canis</u> infection and a number of allergies found in children. Research suggests that infection with this worm can exacerbate allergic manifestations, such as asthma and eczema. This emphasises the important need for regular worming of dogs with effective products.

ENDOPARASITE INFECTIONS FROM OVERSEAS

Now that dogs generally, and breeding bitches particularly, can travel to and from overseas countries under the Pet Travel Scheme (PETS), there is a real risk that some endoparasite infections, which have hitherto not been a problem in the UK, could be unwittingly introduced into this country. Some of these 'exotic' diseases of dogs are of special importance because they can also affect people; they are called, in technical terms, 'zoonoses'.

In this respect, it should be noted that PETS is designed to protect people in the UK, not animals. Medication prescribed under the scheme does not protect animals from tick-borne diseases, because the legality is simply to treat dogs no more than 48 hours before entering or re-entering the UK.

Some details relating to those diseases that are of particular concern are noted below (see table 6). Regular breeders who travel overseas to show their breeding stock or to have a bitch mated, and those who import breeding stock must be aware of the implications of these infections, and also those caused by ectoparasites (see Ectoparasites, page 100).

From a practical point of view, it is advisable for breeders to consult their veterinary surgeon to obtain suitable products and advice on dosage regimes in respect of prophylactic *(preventive)* medication – against endoparasite infections *before* travel. It also makes sense to seek veterinary advice concerning medication for dogs *after* entry into the UK to ensure

TABLE 6: ENDOPARASITE INFECTIONS FROM OVERSEAS

Disease	Cause	Method of transmission	Incubation period
Erlichiosis	A rickettsial blood-borne parasite most commonly *Ehrlichia canis*.	Through tick vectors (carriers). Dogs are infected when bitten by a tick carrying the parasite.	8-20 days post-infection for acute disease, but several weeks or even months post-infection in sub-clinical cases.
Babesiosis	Blood-borne protozoal parasites *Babesia gibsoni* and *B. canis*.	Through blood-sucking ticks.	2-35 days. The infection may lie dormant without signs (latent) for a prolonged period.
Hepato-zoonosis	A coccidia – *Hepatozoon canis*.	Ingestion of the tick vector.	Unclear. Possibly variable.
Leishmaniasis*	An intracellular protozoal parasite.	Sandfly vector. Endemic in many Mediterranean areas. People can be infected by sandfly bites or through contact with infected animals. Of great public health importance.	1 month – 7 years!
Brucellosis*	A bacterium – *Brucella canis*.	Venereally or by ingestion of infected aborted material. Following infection	Unknown.

Signs	Diagnosis	Treatment/prevention
Weakness, fever, then bleeding from the nose, bloodstained urine, eye disease and death.	Examination of blood smears and other laboratory tests needed to confirm a tentative diagnosis.	Antibiotic medication for at least 14 days. Recovery likely if treated promptly and appropriately. Prevention of tick infection before and during overseas travel. No vaccine is available currently.
Fever, bloodstained urine, anaemia, jaundice, death.	Microscopic examination of blood films and other blood tests to confirm diagnosis.	Anti-protozoal drugs: some not available in the UK. Prevention of tick infection before and during overseas travel. No vaccine is currently available in the UK.
Chronic intermittent fever, stiffness, pain, diarrhoea, cough, nasal discharge.	Based on signs. Blood tests, examination of blood smears and microscopic examination of muscle tissue.	Treatment is difficult and may not be effective. Prevention of tick infection before and during overseas travel. No vaccine is currently available in the UK.
Enlarged lymph nodes, eye disease, kidney disease, arthritis, skin disease, weight loss.	Laboratory tests on blood or tissue samples.	No vaccine is currently available. Condition appears to resolve but relapses occur. Prolonged medication with two compounds is currently recommended but a cure is unlikely. Use of fly repellents is important.
In dogs, epididymitis, scrotal enlargement, dermatitis. Not usually a severe illness, but can cause	Laboratory tests on blood serum, or culture of an organism.	Antibiotic medication. Recommended that infected animals are neutered to prevent

TABLE 6: ENDO-PARASITE INFECTIONS FROM OVERSEAS

Disease	Cause	Method of transmission	Incubation period
Brucellosis* *(continued)*		the organism can persist in body cells. Human infection can result from handling infected aborted material.	
Echinococcosis*	A tapeworm.	Worm segments eaten by animals develop into cysts in the lungs, liver, brain and other organs. Dogs are infected by eating tissue containing hydatid cysts. People can be infected by eating food (especially vegetables) contaminated by faeces from infected dogs.	The cysts may remain in intermediate hosts for as long as 29 years! Ripe segments appear in faeces 7-8 weeks after infection.
Heartworm infection*	A large (up to 30 cm/12 in long) roundworm *Dilofilaria immitis,* present in the right side of the heart and adjacent vessels.	Transmitted by mosquitoes. The adult female worms shed live larval worms (microfilariae) into the blood. These are sucked up by mosquitoes, develop in the insect and migrate to the salivary glands. They are 'injected' into dogs when the mosquito bites. Not endemic in the UK at this time, as summers are not consistently warm enough.	Microfilariae appear in the blood about 6 months after infection.

*Note: Diseases marked * are classed as zoonoses, i.e. diseases of animals that can also affect people.*

Signs	Diagnosis	Treatment/prevention
septicaemia and spinal disease. Conception failure in bitches. Foetal resorption and abortion.		the spread of infection.
The tapeworm itself is not a pathogen in dogs but the cysts it produces cause a serious problem in people, sheep and cattle. If the cysts develop in the brain or other vital organs in people, death may result.	Examination of faecal samples from dogs.	Dogs must be treated for this infection before entering the UK under the Pet Travel Scheme (PETS).
People can be infected with this parasite but this occurs only extremely rarely. In people, the worms cause lesions in the lung, they do not lodge in the heart as in dogs. In dogs, the main signs of infection are coughing and tiredness after exercise. Blood clots can cause lung lesions, and pneumonia can result. Usually infection results in chronic and persistent coughing and congestive heart failure.	Signs and history. Specific blood tests and imaging of heart and lungs using radiography or ultrasound.	Products for prevention are available in the UK – and should be used before and during overseas travel. Treatment is complicated and hazardous.

that these new infections are properly contained. This is *not* something that can be tackled without professional help. Temporary isolation while medication is undertaken is a wise precaution in breeding kennels.

Finally, any dog who falls ill after returning from an overseas visit for whatever purpose, business or pleasure, should be taken without delay to a veterinary surgeon for a full clinical examination, and possibly tests, so that the cause of the problem can be identified positively and the correct medication prescribed.

ECTOPARASITE INFECTIONS

FLEAS
It makes sense for all breeders, casual and regular, to regularly inspect their pet or breeding stock for the presence of fleas. If you do find fleas or any flea excrement – like black grains of sand – it is important to take action at once to control them on all stock and, just as importantly, in your house, car or kennels. Otherwise you may create a hatchery of fleas that will be with you for a long time. A well-planned anti-flea strategy is particularly important for regular breeders whose breeding bitches and stud dogs are housed in kennels.

LIFE CYCLE
Adult fleas spend most of their life on their hosts. They lay eggs on the dog and these subsequently fall into crevices anywhere between skirting boards, carpets and cracks between the seats and arms of upholstered chairs and car seats etc. The eggs develop in the environment into larvae and then pupae. This process may take only three to four weeks in warm, humid climates, but can take several months in the UK.

The pupae lie dormant, sometimes for months, only to be triggered to hatch into adult fleas by some vibration in association with the right conditions of temperature and humidity. It is important that your pet bitch or breeding stock does not become infested, since dogs can become sensitive to flea bites, and the resulting skin condition can be time-consuming and costly to cure. Indeed, in some cases it may only be possible to control the skin rash on a temporary basis and permanent medication may be required.

Flea bite dermatitis is one of the most common skin problems in dogs. Nowadays it has become especially important throughout the year – no doubt, largely because many more houses have central heating. Fleas can also carry the minute larvae of the common tapeworm, *Diplydium caninum* (see pages 92-94).

FIGURE 16: LIFE CYCLE OF THE FLEA

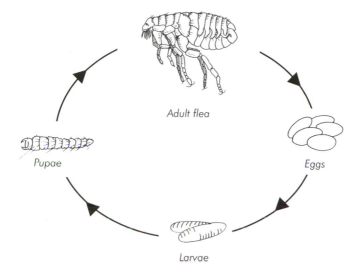

Adult flea

Pupae

Eggs

Larvae

DIAGNOSIS

To find out if a bitch or other breeding stock has fleas, look for small, flattened, brown, elongated, wingless insects! They run over the dog's skin through the hair and jump when they are off the animal. They may be difficult to spot in dogs that groom themselves meticulously. Look particularly around the neck and at the base of the tail of all dogs in the house or kennel.

If you think fleas may be present but you can't find evidence, see your vet. Most likely, the vet will comb the dog and look for the black flea dirts, which are only the size of grains of sand, and which leave a tell-tale red/brown mark when placed on damp blotting paper. This is a procedure that regular breeders can carry out themselves with advantage. In dogs that are hypersensitive to flea bites, there may be just a simple papular rash on the abdomen. But in severe cases, the skin on the back becomes thickened, folded and more darkly coloured.

TREATMENT

Many insecticidal products are available from pet shops and chemists, but it makes sense to talk to your vet, who will advise whether sprays, insecticidal collars, tablets, 'spot-on' or injectable products or powders are most appropriate. Be sure to seek advice on how frequently they should be used to kill existing fleas and prevent re-infection.

PREVENTION

A number of very effective products are also available for use in the environment. They contain a short-acting insecticide, which will kill adult fleas, and a longer-acting compound, which will prevent flea eggs hatching and larvae maturing into adults, thus breaking the whole cycle. They can give as long as seven months' protection when used as directed. Your vet will advise the most cost-effective anti-flea campaign for your circumstances.

TABLE 7: FLEAS – THE ESSENTIAL FACTS

• It is a myth that fleas exist only where there's dirt and disease. Central heating and carpeting provide an environment where fleas thrive.
• Fleas are armour-plated, wingless insects about 2-3 mm long. They are renowned for their ability to jump huge distances for their size.
• The most common flea on dogs is the cat flea, which rejoices in the scientific name *Ctenocephalides felis*.
• Adult fleas spend virtually all of their life on their host. The intermediate stages, larvae and pupae, develop in crevices in kennels, in furnishings, between floorboards, and around the edge of fitted carpets.
• Female fleas can lay as many as 400-500 eggs, which are visible to the naked eye. The eggs develop into larvae and then pupae, which can remain dormant for up to a year before hatching into adult fleas.
• The presence of fleas in dogs is not the only cause of excessive scratching.
• Dogs can pick up tapeworms by swallowing fleas – see under *Dipylidium caninum*.
• A number of very effective products are available these days that can be used to kill adult fleas on dogs. Others have been developed that can be used very successfully in the environment to kill fleas and to prevent the development of eggs, pupae and larvae into adult fleas.

LICE *(TRICHODECTES CANIS)*

LIFE CYCLE
Adult lice feed on skin and lay eggs on hair. These hatch into young lice, which resemble the adults. Lice cannot exist off their host for more than a few days – infection is spread, therefore, by close contact between animals.

DIAGNOSIS
The presence of light-brown, fat, wingless insects with short legs that move slowly on the skin surface and that lay eggs (nits) stuck to the animal's hair, particularly around the neck and ears. Dogs with lice will scratch frequently at the area where the insects are to be found. Severe infections may cause anaemia in young puppies.

TREATMENT
Regular treatment of infected dogs with an insecticide is required, and it makes sense to comb and wash away the nits. Since lice breed on an animal, there is less need to pay attention to the environment than is the case with a flea infection.

TICKS

SPECIES AND THEIR IMPORTANCE
Many different species, both indigenous in the UK and present in overseas countries, can affect dogs. They are important because they can be involved in the transmission of a number of infectious agents (see Table 6, pages 96-99).

LIFE CYCLE
Dogs become infected by coming in contact with nymphs or adults, which have hatched from eggs laid by adult ticks that have left their natural hosts (deer, sheep and hedgehogs), and that climb on to blades of grass and shrubs, waiting for a suitable host to pass.

DIAGNOSIS
Brownish-white, rounded spider-like 'acarids', which may, when engorged, reach the size of a bean or pea. The adult forms lie attached to the skin by their heads, which are firmly buried in the epidermis (the outer layer of the skin). Most dogs will tolerate an adult tick or two without showing any signs. Indeed, it is common for these parasites to be noticed only during routine grooming.

TREATMENT

Adult ticks should be removed by using a proper tick-removing tool or hook available from vets. Ticks should not be handled directly. Other methods of removal may lead to increased injection of toxins from the tick and/or bacterial infections into the bite. If in doubt, seek veterinary assistance.

CHEYLETIELLA MITES

LIFE CYCLE

A small parasite that is just visible to the naked eye, the mite lives on the surface of the skin and lays eggs that stick to the hair. The whole life cycle, which lasts about 21 days, is spent on the host.

DIAGNOSIS

Mostly the mite causes few signs in dogs, but heavy infections can result in marked skin scaling. The mites themselves, together with their eggs and the scurf they produce, has been called 'walking dandruff', and is seen most frequently on the animal's back. Cheyletiella mites can cause an irritating rash in people.

TREATMENT

Treatment of infected dogs is relatively simple but should be under veterinary supervision. One spray-on product can be used on puppies only two days of age where this is considered necessary.

MANGE MITES

Two mange mites – *Demodex canis* and *Sarcoptes scabei* – are responsible for causing skin disease in dogs.

DEMODECTIC MANGE

D. canis mites exist normally in small numbers in canine hair follicles. In certain circumstances, which are not fully understood, these mites multiply dramatically and cause severe inflammation of the skin and hair loss. Usually the skin lesions are localised, but the condition may become generalised, erupting over the whole body and be complicated by secondary bacterial infection. Surprisingly, dogs suffering from demodectic mange do not scratch.

SARCOPTIC MANGE

S. scabei mites are invisible to the naked eye. They burrow superficially into the skin, causing intense irritation and frantic scratching. The areas most commonly affected are under the thighs and forelegs and the edges of the ears. Dogs of all ages and all breeds may be affected. Sarcoptic mites found on dogs are contagious to people, causing a transient skin disease.

TREATMENT
The treatment of demodectic mange is controversial but generally includes the use of insecticides administered twice weekly, supplemented by nutritional support (attention to diet). Some cases eventually recover spontaneously and the prognosis is generally good. Dogs with the pustular form are usually given long-term antibiotic therapy. The use of greasy ointments and corticosteroids is contraindicated. Thus treatment should only be undertaken under veterinary guidance.

Treatment for sarcoptic mange (scabies) needs to be under veterinary guidance. Medication is complicated by the fact that the life cycle of the mite is about three weeks, and re-infection from contaminated bedding can occur. A number of different ectoparasiticides effectively kill the mites, but their administration needs to continue for at least four weeks. Usually corticosteroids are given initially to alleviate the intense irritation and to help the skin lesions heal. Canine scabies papules on humans usually respond promptly to topical medication.

DIAGNOSING ECTOPARASITIC SKIN DISEASES
Ectoparasite infection is probably the major cause of skin disease in dogs. Because the signs are not specific to any one cause, veterinary help should be sought if any skin lesions or signs of irritation are shown by dogs. This will ensure that a proper diagnosis of the cause can be made and the most effective treatment prescribed. This often involves the microscopic examination of skin scrapings.

It is helpful to have to hand a good history of the case, noting details of the signs shown and their time of onset and duration, and whether they are affected by particular events, surroundings or dietary changes. Detail relating to the dog's environment, particularly the bedding used and possible contact with other animals, can also be of help in diagnosis. Finally, it is important to inform the veterinary surgeon if any person in contact with affected dogs is also showing signs of skin disease.

TREATING ECTOPARASITIC SKIN DISEASES
Many very effective novel anti-ectoparasitic compounds are available these days for use in dogs in a variety of products presented as 'spot-

on's', sprays, insecticidal collars and oral products. Although a number can be bought 'over the counter' from chemists and pet shops, it is sensible to obtain veterinary advice so that the most cost-effective product for your needs is chosen and the most appropriate treatment regime is advised for your circumstances.

ECTOPARASITES AND OVERSEAS TRAVEL

As noted in connection with endoparasite infections, ticks are involved in the transmission of a number of the exotic diseases described in Table 6 (pages 96-99). Many of the species of tick, and a number of endoparasite infections that may be encountered overseas, are not, at present, endemic in the UK. Thus, special precautions need to be taken in respect of breeding animals (dogs and bitches) who are being sent to, or returning from, foreign parts. In particular, good preventative medication should be undertaken, coupled possibly with a short period of isolation (quarantine).

Similar precautions should also be undertaken when dogs return to the kennels after having been in contact with animals from overseas, as can occur, for example, at international dog shows, such as Crufts in the UK and Westminster in the US.

DOGS GOING OVERSEAS

Whether a dog is going overseas, either temporarily or to stay, our advice to breeders is always to worm their animals under veterinary guidance before travelling and apply products containing long-acting ectoparasiticides that are effective particularly against ticks. Your veterinary surgeon will be able to advise you on suitable dosage regimes.

DOGS RETURNING FROM OVERSEAS

All these animals will, under the PETS regulations, have been wormed and treated for ticks 24-48 hours before leaving the overseas country. However, it is sensible to isolate such animals for about seven days on their return and to undertake further anti-parasitic medication under veterinary guidance with effective products. It should be noted, however, that such actions may be too late, since they will not be effective against any exotic diseases that have already been contracted. In this context, the recommendation given on page 95 and 100, in relation to dogs that fall ill after coming from overseas, is particularly important.

Finally. it is worth noting that the possible changing disease situation in the UK, which has arisen since the six-month quarantine period for imported dogs from a number of countries is no longer mandatory, has complicated the regulations relating to the export of dogs to some countries, such as Australia. Furthermore, some diseases that are not currently seen in the UK may become a problem in the future as a result of climate change.

INHERITED DISEASES AND CONDITIONS

As a result of recent advances in veterinary medicine, a number of diseases and conditions in dogs have been identified as being inherited. However, the precise mode of inheritance still needs to be established in most cases.

In order to throw more light on this matter, many breed clubs are co-operating with veterinary researchers and, hopefully, this will lead to a better understanding, and possibly the elimination of, these conditions from a number of breeds. Ideally, both regular and occasional breeders should keep in touch with their breed club to familiarise themselves with any investigations, tests and eradication projects that are being carried out in respect of their breed.

In all cases, the onus is on breeders not to repeat any mating that has lead to the offspring having *any* condition that is *considered* to be inherited and which occurs in their particular breed or line. Where eradication schemes exist, e.g. hip dysplasia, only stock confirmed to be clear should be used for breeding.

Hereditary problems may affect:

- The skeleton, including the jaw, the spine and the joints, e.g. hip dysplasia
- The eyes – malformation and possibly blindness
- The heart – structure (anatomy) and function
- The ears – deafness and anatomical defects
- The nervous system – e.g. epilepsy
- The blood – e.g. bleeding disorders
- Temperament – behavioural abnormalities.

Unfortunately, a number of the more common defects seen in many breeds are sometimes not taken sufficiently seriously by breeders. Indeed, some conditions, like undershot jaws for example, may even be an accepted conformation for the breed. Breeders should, on all but the exceptional situation, avoid breeding from stock that have – and that produce – such malformations as large umbilical or inguinal hernias, deformed eyelids, slipping patellas (kneecaps), and cryptorchidism. Morally this is undoubtedly the right course of action, if only because these conditions can possibly lead to affected dogs suffering and cause the new owner worry and expense in having the condition corrected surgically.

Thinking long-term is really the only sensible option, and it is wise to have all litters checked by a veterinary surgeon so that any of these inherited defects can be identified early.

Currently there are schemes administered jointly by the British Veterinary Association and the Kennel Club aimed at eradicating hip dysplasia (set up in 1978), some eye conditions and elbow dysplasia.

Hip dysplasia is particularly important in:
- German Shepherd Dogs
- Golden Retrievers
- Great Danes
- Labrador Retrievers
- Old English Sheepdogs
- Rottweilers
- Rough Collies

The breeds most susceptible to inherited eye conditions include:
- Smooth, Rough and Border Collies
- Basset Hounds
- Cavalier King Charles Spaniels
- Cocker Spaniels
- English Springer Spaniels
- Miniature and Toy Poodles
- Golden Retrievers
- Irish Setters
- Labradors

Heart problems are quite often seen in:
- Cavalier King Charles Spaniels
- Boxers
- Newfoundlands

Breeders who produce litters of the breeds noted above are strongly advised to consult with their veterinary surgeon so that the most effective course of action and breeding programme can be devised and followed.

Novice breeders are advised to contact their breed club to identify any particular inherited problems within the breed, and to establish whether any screening schemes are in existence to monitor them. For example, heart conditions are being monitored in Cavaliers and Boxers. Veterinary surgeons will also be able to give guidance regarding which inherited conditions are a problem in any breed.

Finally, in relation to deafness, which occurs quite commonly in Dalmatians and white dogs, particularly white Boxers and Bull Terriers, puppies may be tested for hearing at the Animal Health Trust at Newmarket at eight weeks of age.

CHAPTER 8

SHAPING A PUPPY'S BEHAVIOUR

Quite recently, the fact has been highlighted that more dogs are destroyed each year as a result of unacceptable behaviour than die of infectious disease. Such behaviour can be largely prevented by full and careful habituation and socialisation, and the application of modern training methods very early in puppyhood.

THE BREEDER'S ROLE
There is no doubt that prevention of inappropriate behaviour is much easier and more effective than attempts to cure established behaviours, such as aggression or destructiveness. It will be obvious, therefore, that all breeders have an important role to play, since the way puppies are raised in the first weeks of their lives is of great importance in respect of their future behaviour and temperament.

STAGES IN A PUPPY'S DEVELOPMENT
Dog behaviourists have identified that puppies go through a number of critical stages during their development (see Table 8). In particular, the first 12 weeks of their life is of special importance.

TABLE 8: KEY STAGES OF PUPPY DEVELOPMENT

STAGE OF DEVELOPMENT	WEEKS												
	1	2	3	4	5	6	7	8	9	10	11	12	13
Neonatal period	▨	■	■	■	▨								
Primary habituation/ socialisation			▨	■	■	■	■	▨					
General habituation/ socialisation							▨	■	■	■	■	▨	▨
Critical period for sensitivity								▨	■	■	■	■	▨

KEY

■ Average start, end and duration of stage

▨ These areas are included to take into account breed and individual puppy variations

Note: the duration of these events is variable between the breeds and individuals of the same breed.

NEONATAL PERIOD

This lasts from 2-4 weeks of age ± 1 week. During this time, puppies are looked after principally by their mother, but some interaction by breeders is needed, mainly to ensure that all the members of a litter are sucking well and that they are defecating and urinating normally.

PRIMARY AND GENERAL HABITUATION/SOCIALISATION PERIODS

This occurs from 4-12 weeks of age ± 1 week. This period is important, as puppies are at the height of their learning ability. Of course, dogs go on learning throughout their lives, but these formative weeks are the most critical.

CRITICAL PERIOD FOR SENSITIVITY
The critical period for sensitivity is from 9-12 weeks of age ± 1 week. This is significant because it is during this stage in a puppy's development that fearful experiences can become firmly imprinted for life.

THE IMPORTANCE OF THESE DEVELOPMENTAL PERIODS
From the facts noted above, it will be obvious that breeders have a very important role to play if full advantage is to be taken of these vital early weeks in a puppy's life. This is particularly the case if puppies are homed late, perhaps because finding buyers or homing is proving difficult or, in the case of pedigree dogs belonging to regular breeders, if the litter is being kept back so that those pups with the best characteristics can be more reliably identified and retained for show or breeding purposes. It is relevant to note that, since 1999, registered breeders are, by law, not allowed to sell puppies before they are eight weeks of age.

All this means that owners of new puppies may often have only three to four weeks in which to effectively habituate and socialise their newly acquired puppy, to complete house-training, and to start training it to respond to basic commands. It is essential, therefore, and especially if puppies are not to be homed at six weeks of age, that breeders start this process to ensure that the pups have a proper start in life, thus reducing the risk of bad habits becoming established. If this action is not taken, there is a real risk of owners being disappointed in their dog's behaviour and some may even consider returning newly acquired dogs to the breeder as being unsatisfactory.

Hopefully, the information given in this chapter will help in two ways. First, we aim to give breeders some direction and to clarify the role they need to play. Secondly, the details outlined will, we hope, be of help to breeders when they come to inform new puppy owners about how best to manage their pet with regard to future behaviour.

In essence, two fundamental matters need to be considered:
• How dogs learn
• How dogs can be taught.

HOW DOGS LEARN
Understanding how dogs learn is a fundamental necessity if they are to be taught to be well mannered and properly integrated into society. Learning is usually defined as a 'change in behaviour brought about as a result of previous experience'. Essentially, dogs learn by habituation/ socialisation and association.

HABITUATION/SOCIALISATION

As part of a survival strategy, nature ensures that newborn animals perceive all new experiences as being potentially threatening and that evasive action should be taken. Habituation means, in simple terms, 'the loss of such an unlearned, natural, inherent behaviour'. This comes about as the animal learns that the particular experience (stimulus) is not, after all, a cause for concern. For example, puppies are naturally fearful of loud noises, but if they are encountered every day, or at least frequently, without untoward result, the puppies will become accustomed to such noises and ignore them. The natural response of fearfulness will be lost or at least reduced.

This is how puppy 'habituation' (becoming accustomed to sounds and objects) and 'socialisation' (accepting people and other animals) works, and its importance will be obvious. If dogs are to fit into society, it is essential that they learn that there is no need to be fearful of the noise of washing machines or vacuum cleaners, or worried about postmen, dustmen and the like.

ASSOCIATION

Associative learning can involve conscious thought (in technical terms this is called instrumental conditioning), or involuntary reflex actions (this is termed classical conditioning).

INSTRUMENTAL CONDITIONING

This is the main way dogs learn, and simply means that a behaviour is determined by the result it brings. Or, put another way, dogs learn essentially by trial and error. By repetition, dogs learn that certain actions will bring a pleasurable response or an unpleasant result. If a response to a stimulus or command results in a pleasurable experience within 0.5-1 second (so that the dog can link the two events), the dog will most likely respond in the same way again if the stimulus or command is repeated.

If, on the other hand, the response results in a prompt unpleasant experience, such as pain or possibly simply being ignored by the owner, the dog will tend to avoid responding in the same way again. After a relatively few such unrewarding experiences, the dog will realise that the particular response does not 'pay off' and the action will be 'extinguished' from the dog's repertoire.

CLASSICAL CONDITIONING

An example of this form of learning is illustrated in the classical experiment carried out in dogs by the Russian physiologist Pavlov. He showed that salivation is an automatic reflex response whenever food comes into contact with the mouth. He went on to find that if a bell is rung consistently at the same time as food is given, eventually dogs will learn that the sound of the bell heralds the arrival of food and they begin to salivate. They will do this to the sound of the bell even when food is not forthcoming.

A more practical illustration of classical conditioning involves house-training puppies. If puppies are taken outside consistently when they are likely to want to go to the toilet (either urinate or defecate) they will quite soon associate going out with the reflex body action. If *at the same time as* the puppy 'performs' the owner whistles in an undulating way, the puppy will eventually 'learn' to urinate or defecate when it hears that particular whistle. This method was used in the past by grooms to encourage their charges to urinate outside the horse box to minimise the need to 'muck out' – or at least to make it less arduous.

TEACHING AIDS
In simple terms, owners have four aids or methods (tools) that can be used to teach dogs. If these are applied correctly, consistently and promptly, dogs will learn to respond in the desired way surprisingly quickly.

FOOD
The use of small pieces of delectable food. A coveted tidbit, such as pieces of meat or cheese, can be used very effectively as a reward for a desired response to a command. It should be noted, however, that since the reward needs to be given very promptly, wrapped food is of little use! The dog will not make the association between the command and his response if he has to wait for the reward to be unwrapped or retrieved from the depth of a coat pocket!

PRAISE
Dogs will regard as praise any form of attention (including petting, stroking etc.). They will soon learn to respond in the desired way when a command results in pleasure, especially if accompanied by verbal encouragement. However, it is important to take care that any action that the dog may perceive as praise is not made *inadvertently* when the dog is misbehaving. If this is done, the inappropriate behaviour will soon become part of the dog's repertoire! This is, in fact, one of the major causes of inappropriate behaviour in dogs. Once the owner realises the significance of their actions and stops them, the behaviour will usually quickly become extinguished.

CHASTISEMENT

Chastisement is controlled punishment. Essentially, punishment can take two forms: administering a painful stimulus and withdrawal of privileges (see below).

> *If there is any doubt which of the training aid/tools mentioned above should be used, it is best to turn away and ignore the behaviour. It is far better to do nothing than to get it wrong. Relying on an inappropriate behaviour being extinguished (forgotten) is often a good safe option in many dogs, and especially in those that have a tendency to dominance.*

The administration of a painful stimulus

In this context, the severity of punishment will need to be varied according to the pet's size and temperament. Punishment of this nature must never be cruel, nor should it be used in temper. Ideally, it can be helpful to give the dog the chance to adopt an alternative behaviour, not compatible with the undesired behaviour, which will bring a reward. If punishment is used, it is most important to follow the rules noted below.

Because punishment may be associated in the dog's mind with the person administering the punishment rather than with the unwanted behaviour, it can – if not properly used – result in fear or aggression. Furthermore, the dog may come to think the response is only inappropriate in the presence of the person administering the punishment.

So-called 'magic punishment' can be very effective indeed. A suitable object, such as a bean bag thrown from a hiding place, which strikes the dog *while the crime is actually being committed,* is particularly useful in many cases. The dog does not link the punishment with the owner (the dog believes that he is being punished by the environment), and it is immediate and unpredictable.

A single application of this method was sufficient to stop a Dobermann, who had developed a habit of 'raiding' handbags left on the floor, from ever committing the act again. This example also highlights the value of 'set-up' situations, where the owner anticipates the wrong-doing and is ready and prepared to administer the punishment *as the 'sin' is being committed.*

The withdrawal of something pleasurable

Simply ignoring the dog, giving him no attention at all and showing your displeasure by your body language, will often be sufficient to teach the dog that there is no point in repeating the undesirable behaviour. If this is not enough, banishing the dog to a room on his own and ignoring him (in other words, social isolation or 'sending him to Coventry' for a short while) can also be effective, and the dog will soon learn that the inappropriate behaviour does not 'pay off'.

Rules governing the use of chastisement

- Apply the punishment consistently, fairly and without delay.
- Make the punishment appropriate to the crime.
- Use punishment that is strong enough to disrupt the undesirable behaviour, but is not prolonged and does not cause suffering.
- Do not punish shy, nervous dogs or puppies less than 12 weeks of age; in such cases, a firm "No", accompanied by disapproving body language, will usually be enough.
- A quick, hard tap on the nose may be effective in the case of larger dogs, but care should be taken that such an action is not confused with play, since that can be completely counterproductive and may even encourage aggression or anxiety.
- If you have any doubts about the appropriateness of punishment, it is better to ignore the behaviour. If in any doubt, apply social isolation.

RE-ENFORCEMENT

Re-enforcement means establishing and maintaining a learnt behaviour.

- Learning is achieved more quickly if the response is rewarded (reinforced) every time a command is obeyed promptly and correctly.
- Intermittent, random, strong reinforcement (big rewards) are most effective in *maintaining* a desired behaviour. Think of the one-armed bandit – very occasional good rewards out of the blue. Gamblers are 'programmed' to go on pulling the handle.
- If no rewards are given, the behaviour will extinguish – the response will be forgotten.
- If a reward becomes associated with a neutral stimulus (e.g. a sound, smell or visual stimulus that is previously of no significance to the dog), the previously neutral stimulus can itself be used to reinforce a learnt behaviour. Such a stimulus is termed a secondary reinforcer. In clicker training the click becomes associated with a reward, thus allowing a click to be used very promptly to reward a desired response. Specific gestures, or the undulating whistle noted earlier, can be used in a similar way but, again, care must be taken that they are not used inadvertently to reward an inappropriate act by the dog.

IN SUMMARY

Dogs will learn:

- To repeat an action if it is rewarded.
- If behaviour results in 'punishment', to try an alternative behaviour in the hope that the new behaviour will bring some reward.
- If a behaviour is not rewarded or is ignored, then it is best forgotten; it will be extinguished from the dog's repertoire.

PRACTICAL PUPPY MANAGEMENT

Properly planned, careful habituation and socialisation is of extreme importance if pet owners are to have an 'ideal dog' of which they can be justifiably proud. It is in this context that breeders have an important role and obligation.

PRIMARY HABITUATION/SOCIALISATION PERIOD

During this phase in their development (4-7 weeks ± 1 week), puppies should be habituated (accustomed) to the sounds they will encounter later in life, such as the sound of vacuum cleaners, dishwashers, washing machines, the clatter of cutlery and crockery, the telephone ringing and the flushing of toilets etc. To achieve this, it is more appropriate if puppies are reared within the house rather than in kennels. Where this is not possible, the use of sound CDs to prevent the development of sound phobias is worth considering. For further information, see Appendix 3.

During this time it is important that the breeder also begins to familiarise the pup to being handled all over. This should be done purposefully and regularly, at least twice daily from week 4 until the puppy goes to its new home.

In this period the puppy should also be socialised by meeting children and selected adults in the house; maybe to potential purchasers. During the latter part of this period, the breeder should start the house-training process (see later). We recognise that meeting all the situations noted above is not easy for regular breeders with many breeding bitches, and with large breeds that are housed in outside kennels after three to four weeks of age. It is, however, most important for such breeders to make sure that as many of the conditions described are catered for, even if it does prove time-consuming. Frequent visits to the kennels, and handling all the puppies regularly and thoroughly, is most important. A special effort should be made to ensure that the puppies get used to as wide a variety of quiet and loud sounds as possible.

GENERAL HABITUATION/SOCIALISATION PERIOD

In order that this critical period in a puppy's development (8-12 weeks ± 1 week) can be maximised, it is advisable that puppies should go to their new homes from six weeks of age, although, as noted earlier, this is not always practical or possible.

This all-important process, habituation and socialisation, which can make or mar the chance of the puppy becoming an 'ideal dog', requires much thought and dedication to ensure that each new experience is a 'happy' one. There is the need to go slowly and carefully and to plan ahead.

Focus on familiarising the puppy to the sounds and different types of people as noted in Table 9, below. In the later stages of this period, if the puppy is taken outside, the opportunity should be used to introduce it cautiously to specific objects, such as cars and bicycles, and to other animals, such as cats and horses.

TABLE 9: SOUNDS, OBJECTS, PEOPLE AND SITUATIONS WITH WHICH DOGS SHOULD BE FAMILIARISED

People	Sounds	Objects	Animals
Children playing loudly	Carpet sweepers	Balls	Cats and other pets
Crowded streets	Dishwashers	Bicycles	Cattle
Dustmen	Fireworks	Buses	Chickens
Joggers	Lorries reversing	Cars	Goats
Men and women (including vets!)	Police, fire and ambulance sirens	Lorries	Horses
People with sticks	Power tools	Post boxes	Other dogs
People carrying loads	Telephones	Phone boxes	Sheep
Postmen	Television/radio	Steps and stairways	Wild birds and wild animals
Rustling clothes	Vacuum cleaners	Trains	
	Washing machines	Traffic lights	

Finally, it should be noted that although habituation and socialisation is particularly important between the ages of 8-12 weeks as mentioned earlier, it should be an ongoing process throughout a dog's life. The experiences should be made as broad as possible by including towns and countryside and a variety of forms of transport.

CRITICAL PERIOD FOR SENSITIVITY

This stage in the puppy's development (9-12 weeks ± 1 week) is significant, since any experience that causes acute fear at this time may make a dog anxious, shy or very fearful of similar occurrences for the rest of his life. This is particularly likely to be the case with puppies that already have an introvert temperament. Dominant, exuberant dogs are much less likely to be affected in this way.

It is particularly important to think ahead and distract puppies in some way if anything untoward occurs, such as a very loud noise outside. There is the need, however, to take special care that any anxious behaviour is not being rewarded by too much attention. It is particularly important to pay attention to this matter if puppies are being raised around Fireworks Night or Christmas to prevent the establishment of a phobia of loud noises and flashes of light.

HOUSE-TRAINING

Breeders can help purchasers of new puppies by commencing house-training as soon as the puppies are old enough to start being weaned and begin to walk about and leave the nest.

Usually puppies are encouraged by their mothers not to soil the nest itself but to go to an area in the pen, immediately outside their bed, when they need to urinate or defecate. Most commonly this site is covered with a layer of newspaper. However, it is helpful if the pups don't become firmly conditioned to regard newspaper as the right place to go to the toilet. Efforts should be made, therefore, to take the pups outside into the garden – just as soon as they are old enough – to a more suitable place whenever they are likely to want to urinate or defecate. It can be helpful to make use of the bitch's own training. When the puppies follow her out, praise the pups and the bitch. Call the bitch, and, when she comes and the pups follow, give lavish praise to them all. Should the pups go to the toilet when their mother does, give loads and loads of praise.

The steps to success are:
- Be prepared to take all the puppies outside, even if just one shows signs of being restless, starts to circle and begins to crouch.

- Take all the puppies out when they wake after a good sleep, and immediately after they have been fed.
- Make a very conscious effort not to fail in these tasks.
- When outside and the puppies perform, make the undulating whistle or other signal described earlier in this chapter (see page 113). Immediately after they have finished, give them plenty of praise verbally and by petting. Provided that it can be done immediately, giving a small tidbit of food will help to establish and reinforce the desired behaviour more firmly.
- Opinion is divided, but we consider that it is better not to select a particular place in the garden or a specific surface for toilet purposes. To do so could be counterproductive in the long-term. Far better that puppies learn to go anywhere, except maybe the flower beds!
- Finally, anyone who adopts a puppy will need to have the undulating whistle, or other signal that has been used, properly demonstrated to them and to be instructed in its use.

BASIC TRAINING

All dogs need to be trained to respond promptly and properly (using the behaviour modification techniques noted earlier in this chapter) to at least six basic commands, namely:

- **Sit**
- **Down**
- **Stay**
- **Heel**
- **Come**
- **Leave**
- **No**
- **Okay** (to indicate the release following a required response).

Ideally, this should be achieved by the time puppies are 12 to 14 weeks of age, using the behaviour modification techniques noted in this chapter. Breeders should at least start this procedure in puppies that are kept beyond six weeks of age. Lessons on a litter basis are most unlikely to be very effective, and thus puppies must be singled out one at a time for basic training purposes. From a breeder's point of view, it is important to ensure simply that a correct response to a command is rewarded promptly with praise and/or a tidbit of food.

It may be helpful to watch closely what a puppy is doing, and to give it an appropriate command *as it does some act that you want to establish*. If the puppy looks as if it is about to sit, say **"Sit"** and reward the pup when it does. It is surprising how few repetitions are needed to establish a behaviour of this sort.

For further information in respect of dog behaviour modification techniques and training, please see the companion volume to this book – *Puppylopaedia*.

SUMMARY

- Breeders have an extremely important role to play in respect of the habituation and socialisation of puppies. This is especially the case in puppies that are homed after six weeks of age.
- Puppies should be familiarised from four weeks of age to a wide variety of sounds, people, objects and maybe other animals.
- As far as possible, situations that may cause fear need to be avoided in the critical period for sensitivity i.e. when puppies are nine to 12 weeks of age.
- Breeders need to understand how dogs learn, and to be familiar with the modern teaching methods. This will mean that puppies can be given a good start in life and that basic training can be commenced at a young age and be more effectively achieved.
- One final word of caution for regular breeders: many behavioural traits (including the inclination to develop phobic responses as well as aggression, excessive fearfulness and destructive tendencies) may well have an inherent component. Thus, it makes sense to consider very carefully whether it is sensible and fair to breed from bitches who have such undesirable tendencies, or who have produced puppies previously that have had behavioural problems where there is no obvious cause.

APPENDIX 1

DOG BREEDERS AND THE LAW

Dog breeding in the UK is controlled by the Breeding of Dogs Act 1973, the Breeding of Dogs Act 1991 and by the Breeding and Sale of Dogs (Welfare) Act 1999. Essentially, it is an offence for any person to keep a dog breeding establishment without a licence issued by a local authority. Dog breeding is construed under the 1999 Act as the carrying on by any person at premises of any nature (including a private dwelling) a business of breeding dogs with a view to their being sold in the course of such business whether by the keeper thereof or any other person. Local authorities have the power to inspect licensed premises to ensure that:

- The accommodation is suitable in respect of size, construction, the number of occupants, exercising facilities, temperature control, ventilation, lighting and cleanliness.
- The dogs are fed adequately and they have drinking water freely available at all times.
- The dogs are adequately exercised, provided with suitable bedding material, and are not left unattended for prolonged periods of time.
- Precautions are taken to prevent the spread of contagious diseases.
- There are adequate fire precautions.

The Breeding and Sale of Dogs (Welfare) Act 1999 states that registered breeders are not allowed to sell puppies until they are eight weeks of age unless they are sold to a licensed pet shop.

Unregistered breeders are not constrained in this way, although the local authority's building control office can deem that a business is trading at the premises, which requires planning permission and that planning permission is required.

License application forms and further information can be obtained from your local authority (community services).

APPENDIX 2

KENNEL CLUB REGISTRATION

Most purchasers of pedigree dogs and bitches prefer to buy puppies that are registered with the Kennel Club. This is because KC registration generally ensures that the pups have been raised in accordance with a practical code of ethics, and that the chosen dog will be representative of the breed in looks, conformation and temperament. The Kennel Club breed register is only available to those puppies where both the sire and the dam are also registered.

The breeder, that is the owner of the litter's mother, is required to complete an application form, which is available from the Kennel Club on application, for registration of the whole litter. The form may also be downloaded from the Kennel Club website www.the-kennel-club.org.uk. The owner of the litter's sire is required to sign the form. The standard registration fee is currently £12 per puppy.

Ideally, the registration of the puppies should be done promptly so that the document can be made available to the purchasers when the pups are homed. This is also wise since the Kennel Club offers six weeks' free Healthcare Plan insurance to new owners from the date of purchase provided they transfer the puppy's ownership to themselves. As an incentive to breeders to register puppies, the Kennel Club offers to refund the puppy registration fee for each new owner who agrees to continue with the Healthcare Plan annual cover and their Certificate of Insurance. From an animal welfare point of view, this makes a lot of sense.

Breeders who register a litter of puppies with the Kennel Club can simultaneously place them on the Puppy Sale Register for an additional fee of just £15 for the whole litter, regardless of size.

The Kennel Club has produced a very helpful quick-and-easy guide to puppy registration. This can be obtained on application to the Kennel Club at 4a Alton House Office Park, Gatehouse Way, Gatehouse Industrial Area, Aylesbury, Bucks, HP19 8XU, or downloaded from the club's website.

Breeders should alert purchasers of registered puppies to the need to transfer ownership into their own name by completing the registration certificate, which they will have been given. This should be done promptly to ensure that the correct information is recorded on the Club's database. It should be pointed out that only dogs that are registered with the Kennel Club can be shown and used in their turn to breed registered puppies. This is also an appropriate time to inform the new owner of the unique range of benefits offered by the Kennel Club Health Plan, which can give owners peace of mind and the best possible care and protection for their dogs.

The Kennel Club also has an Obedience and Working Trials register. This is open to any dog of any ancestry. Registered dogs may be eligible to compete in Obedience, Working Trials, Agility and Flyball competitions. They are not, however, eligible to compete in Field Trials or Gundog Working Tests.

Finally, the Kennel Club runs a Companion Dog Club. Crossbreed dogs, or non-registered pedigree pups, can be registered and they will be entitled to take up the Kennel Club Health Plan, other benefits and receive three newsletters a year. Over 2,000 clubs and societies are registered by the Kennel Club; these offer a useful introduction to the world of dogs.

APPENDIX 3

USEFUL CONTACTS

DOG TRAINING/BEHAVIOUR

ASSOCIATION FOR THE STUDY OF ANIMAL BEHAVIOUR (ASAB)
82a High Street, Sawston, Cambridge, Cambridgeshire, CB2 4HJ.
Tel: 01223 830665 Web: http://asab.nottingham.ac.uk

ASSOCIATION OF PET BEHAVIOUR COUNSELLORS (APBC)
PO Box 46, Worcester, Worcestershire, WR8 9YS.

Tel: 01386 751151 Fax: 01386 750743 Email: info@apbc.org.uk
Web: www.apbc.org.uk

ASSOCIATION OF PET DOG TRAINERS
PO Box 17, Kempsford, GL7 4WZ.
Tel: 01285 810811
Email: APDToffice@aol.com Web: www.apdt.co.uk

BRITISH INSTITUTE OF PROFESSIONAL DOG TRAINERS (BIPDT)
Bowstone Gate, Nr. Disley, Cheshire, SK12 2AW.
Web: www.bipdt.net

COMPANION ANIMAL BEHAVIOUR THERAPY STUDY GROUP (CABTSG)
The Pet Behaviour Centre, Hillside, Upper Street, Defford, Worcestershire,
WR8 9AB.
Tel: 01386 750615 Email: cabtsg@btinternet.com Web: www.cabtsg.org

COMPANY OF ANIMALS AND ANIMAL BEHAVIOUR CENTRE
Ruxbury Farm, St. Ann's Hill Road, Chertsey, Surrey, KT16 9NL.
Tel: 01932 566696 (Company of Animals)
Tel: 01932 574271 or 01932 574281 (Animal Behaviour Centre)
Email: behaviour@companyofanimals.co.uk or office@companyofanimals.co.uk
Web: www.companyofanimals.co.uk

SOCIETY FOR COMPANION ANIMAL STUDIES (SCAS)
The Blue Cross, Shilton Road, Burford, Oxfordshire, OX18 4PF.
Tel: 01993 825597 Fax: 01993 825598
Email: info@scas.org.uk Web: www.scas.org.uk

WEBSITES DISTRIBUTING SOUND PHOBIA CDs
www.soundscary.com
www.fearoffireworks.com
www.companyofanimals.co.uk

GOVERNMENT

PET TRAVEL SCHEME – DEFRA
(Department for Environment Food and Rural Affairs)
Area 201, 1a Page Street, London, SW1P 4PQ.
Tel: 0870 241 1710 Fax: 020 7904 6834
Email: pets.helpline@defra.gsi.gov.uk
Web: www.defra.gov.uk/animalh/quarantine/index.htm

KENNEL CLUB

HEAD OFFICE
1-5 Clarges Street, Piccadilly, London, W1Y 8AB.
Web: www.the-kennel-club.org.uk
SHOWS AND AWARDS
Tel: 0870 606 6750 Fax: 0207 518 1058

PETLOG (PET IDENTIFICATION SERVICE)
Tel: 0870 606 0751 Email: petlogadmin@the-kennel-club.org.uk

GENERAL ENQUIRIES
4a Alton House, Office Park, Gatehouse Way, Gatehouse Industrial Area, Aylesbury, Buckinghamshire, HP19 8XU.
Tel: 0870 606 6750

VETERINARY ASSOCIATIONS

ANIMAL HEALTH TRUST
Lanwades Park, Kentford, Newmarket, Suffolk, CB8 7UU.
Tel: 08700 502424 Fax: 08700 502425
Email: info@aht.org.uk Web: www.aht.org.uk

BRITISH SMALL ANIMAL VETERINARY ASSOCIATION
Woodrow House, 1 Telford Way, Waterwells Business Park, Quedgley, Gloucestershire, GL2 2AB.
Tel: 01452 726700 Fax: 01452 726701
Email: adminoff@bsava.com Web: www.bsava.com

BRITISH VETERINARY ASSOCIATION
7 Mansfield Street, London, W1G 9NQ.
Tel: 0207 636 6541 Fax: 0207 436 2970
Email: bvahq@bva.co.uk Web: www.bva.co.uk

BRITISH VETERINARY NURSING ASSOCIATION
Suite 11, Shenval House, South Row, Harlow, Essex, CM20 2BD.
Tel: 01279 450567 Fax: 01279 420886
Email: bvna@bvnaoffice.plus.com Web: www.bvna.org.uk

PET HEALTH COUNCIL
1, Bedford Avenue, London. WC1B 3AU.
Tel: 0207 255 5408
Email: phc@grayling.co.uk Web: www.pethealthcouncil.co.uk

ROYAL COLLEGE OF VETERINARY SURGEONS
Belgravia House, 62-64 Horseferry Road, London, SW1P 2AF.
Tel: 0207 222 2001 Fax: 0207 222 2004
Email: admin@rcvs.org.uk Web: www.rcvs.org.uk/

APPENDIX 4

GLOSSARY

Acute — Severe disease with a short course.

An-oestrus — The period of sexual inactivity (rest) in the oestrous cycle.

Antibiotic — A substance produced by micro-organisms that inhibits the growth of, or destroys, bacteria. May be given by injection, by mouth or applied locally. Many are now produced synthetically.

Antigen — Any substance, such as pollen, a bacterium, or a virus, which stimulates the production of antibodies in the blood.

Associative learning — Learning by trial and error.

Benign (tumour) — Slow-growing, non-malignant.

BHS — Beta-haemolytic streptococci – round-shaped bacteria that may cause vaginitis and be involved as a cause of fading puppies.

Body language — Postures and facial expressions used by dogs to communicate with each other.

Bordetella bronchiseptica — A bacterium – one of the causes of Kennel Cough.

Brucellosis — The disease caused by an infection with the bacterium *Brucella canis*.

Canine Coronovirus infection — A viral infection of dogs, causing enteritis.

Canine Distemper — A severe viral infection of dogs not commonly seen nowadays.

Canine Herpes virus infection — A virus infection of dogs, a cause of fading puppies and possibly involved in the cause of Kennel Cough.

Canker (ear) — A lay term for inflammation of the outer ear – technically called *otitis externa*.

Castration — Surgical removal of the male gonads (testicles).

Classical conditioning — A form of associative learning.

Colostrum — The first milk produced by the dam in the first days after giving birth, which contains protective antibodies.

Congenital — Present at birth

Cryptorchidism — Failure of one or both testicles to descend into the scrotum – they are retained in the abdomen.

Cutaneous — Appertaining to the skin.

Cystitis — Inflammation of the urinary bladder.

Defecation — The passing of faeces (excreta, motions).

Demodex canis — A dog mange mite, the cause of demodectic mange.

Dew claw — An extra claw near the wrist (carpus) or below the hock. They are usually removed when puppies are a few days old.

Diabetes mellitus — Lack of insulin production, leading to raised blood sugar levels.

Dipylidium caninum — A tapeworm affecting dogs.

Docking — Shortening the tail, carried out in young puppies – a contentious issue currently.

Dys- — A prefix meaning 'painful' or 'difficult'.

Ectoparasite infections — Infections caused by skin parasites, e.g. fleas, lice, mange mites.

Endocrine glands — Glands that secrete hormones into the blood to act as chemical messengers, which control the function of tissues and organs in the body.

Endoparasite infections — Infections caused by parasites inside the body, e.g. in the blood, intestines or respiratory system.

Enteritis — Inflammation of the intestinal tract.

Entire bitches	Bitches that have not been spayed (neutered).
Extinction (extinguish)	The loss of a learnt behaviour through lack of reward.
Faeces	Excreta from the bowel (motions).
False pregnancy	The signs of pregnancy, nursing and lactation in non-pregnant bitches.
Gingivitis	Inflammation of the gums.
Habituation	To get used to (accustomed to) a stimulus.
Heat	A lay term used to describe the summation of pro oestrus and oestrus. The time when bitches are attractive to dogs and will, in the latter half, 'accept' dogs.
Heredity	The process of passing traits or characteristics from one generation to the next.
Hip dysplasia	Progressive inherited changes in the hip joint with the result that the joint cannot function normally.
History	A description of the signs of illness, noting particularly when they occurred.
Hormone	A chemical messenger produced by an endocrine gland and transported by the blood to a target organ where it will exert its effect (see also Endocrine glands).
Hyper-	A prefix meaning 'excessive'.
Hyperplasia	Excessive growth (of a tissue).
Hypersexual	Oversexed.
Hypertrophy	Increase in the size of an organ or tissue.
Hypo-	A prefix meaning 'deficient/less than', e.g. hypothyroid – an underactive thyroid, resulting in low levels of thyroid hormone in the blood.
Hypoplasia	Incomplete development of an organ or tissue, e.g.vaginal hypoplasia.
Hypothermia	Lowered body temperature.
Hysterectomy	Surgical removal of the uterus (see also Ovariohysterectomy).
Immunity (active)	Antibodies in the blood, produced by the animal itself, stimulated by vaccination, or resulting from exposure to organisms causing disease, e.g. bacteria or viruses.
Immunity (passive)	Antibodies acquired by puppies from their mothers, mostly via the first milk (colostrum), but also while the pups are in the womb.
Inappetence	Reluctance or inability to eat.
Incoordination	Lack of balance – difficulty standing and walking.
Infectious Canine Hepatitis	A virus infection of dogs.
Inguinal hernia	Protrusion of abdominal organs/contents through the inguinal canal in the groin to lie under the skin outside the abdominal muscles.
Inherited	A trait or characteristic passed on from one generation to the next.
Instrumental conditioning	Learning by trial and error – behaviour being determined by the result it brings.
Larva (larvae *pl.*)	An immature stage in the development of some parasites viz. *Toxocara canis*.
Leptospirosis	A bacterial disease caused by *Leptospira canicola* (kidney disease) or *L. icterohaemorrhagiae* (liver disease).
Lesion	A pathological change in a tissue.
Lethargy	Disinclination to move.
Libido	Sex drive.
Lymph nodes (glands)	Glands or nodes scattered throughout the body that become swollen in the case of infection. They act as filters to remove bacteria and other debris from the blood.

Appendix 4

Malignant (tumour)	Severe, life-threatening, capable of spreading.
Mammary tumours	Tumours in the mammary glands.
Mastitis	Inflammation of the mammary glands.
Maternally derived passive antibodies	Antibodies in a puppy's blood stream passed on by the mother, mainly in the first milk (colostrum) but also while in the womb.
Metacestode	An intermediate stage in the flea's life cycle; a larval form.
Metoestrus	Stage of the oestrous cycle that follows heat and precedes an-oestrus.
Metritis	Inflammation of the uterus.
Micro-chip	A small bar-coded pellet implanted under the skin to identify dogs.
Mismating	Unintentional mating. Also called misalliance or mesalliance.
Motions	An alternative word for faeces – dog excrement.
Mucoid	Applied to a discharge, meaning that it is like mucus.
Mucus (n)/ mucous (adj)	A clear, slimy often tenacious fluid produced by a mucous membrane, e.g. the lining of the vagina.
Myometrium	The muscles of the uterus (womb).
Neonatal	Newborn.
Neutering	Removal of the male or female gonads (the testicles or ovaries).
Oestrogen	A female sex hormone produced in the ovaries by the follicles – responsible for sex drive and the female sex characteristics.
Oestrus	The period during heat when the bitch will accept the male.
Ovaries	The female gonads, which produce ova (eggs) and the female sex hormone oestrogen.
Ovariohysterectomy	Surgical removal of the uterus and ovaries – spaying.
Overshot	Malformation of the jaw where the upper teeth protrude forwards beyond those in the lower jaw – the opposite of 'undershot'.
Parvovirus infection	A serious viral infection of dogs.
Passive immunity	Immunity (antibodies) acquired by a puppy from his mother, mainly through ingestion of colostrum (first milk), or, in adult dogs, by the administration of antiserum.
Pathogenesis	The development of a disease process.
Penis	The male copulatory organ.
Perinatal	The period around the time of birth.
Pheromones	A group of chemicals excreted from the external surfaces of animals that are used in communication between members of the same species. They are sometimes referred to as 'social odours' although they cannot be smelt by people. Historically, they have been used to lure insects into traps, using the pheromone produced by females to attract males. A synthetic pheromone DAP (dog-appeasing pheromone) is used to calm anxious dogs.
Phobia	Morbid dislike or excessive fear of a thing or situation.
Poly-	A prefix meaning 'many' or 'increased'.
Polydypsia	Increased thirst.
Polyuria	Passing increased quantities of urine.
Prepuberal	Before puberty.
Prepuce	Loose skin covering the penis.
Prognosis	The expected outcome of a disease.
Prolapse	Protrusion, to the outside, of an abdominal organ, e.g. vaginal prolapse or rectal prolapse.
Proliferation	To grow in size.
Pro oestrus	The first stage of heat, when a bitch is attractive to dogs.
Prophylaxis	Prevention of a disease.
Prostate gland	A gland at the base of the bladder around the urethra in male dogs, which produces a fluid that goes to make up semen.
Prostatic hypertrophy	Enlargement of the prostate gland

Breeding A Litter

Puberty	The time of life when an animal becomes sexually mature.
Punishment	A form of negative reinforcement. Anything that stops a behaviour because it disrupts it and ensures that it does not 'pay off'.
Pupa (pupae *pl.*)	A developmental stage of ectoparasites.
Purulent	Containing pus.
Pyometra	Accumulation of fluid in the uterus, usually occurring one to two months after oestrus. A serious, life-threatening condition.
Pyrexia	Raised body temperature – fever.
Reinforcement	Anything that makes an animal repeat a learnt response.
Sarcoptes scabei	A canine mange mite; the cause of sarcoptic mange.
Season	A lay term to describe when a bitch is 'on heat'.
Separation anxiety	The fear of being left alone.
Socialisation	To get used to (accustomed to) different types of people and situations so that they do not invoke a fearful response.
Spay (spey, spaying)	Surgical sterilisation of a female by removal of the uterus and ovaries – ovariohysterectomy.
Staphylococci	Bacteria that commonly occur, particularly in association with skin disease.
Stimulus	Any event, movement, sound, touch or smell detected by an animal that may generate a reaction.
Streptococci	Commonly occurring bacteria that frequently affect dogs and may be associated, for example, with tonsillitis or vaginitis.
Subclinical	Applied to a disease in which the signs are not obvious on clinical examination.
Syndrome	A set of signs that occur together, indicating a particular condition or disease.
Tartar	The accumulation of a hard deposit on the teeth.
Tenesmus	Painful and ineffective straining – to pass faeces or urine.
Territory marking	Urine deposited by dogs or bitches to denote their presence or to mark out their territory.
Testicles	The male gonads, which produce testosterone (the male sex hormone) and spermatozoa.
Testosterone	The male sex hormone responsible for male sex characteristics and libido.
Toxaemia	The spread of bacterial products (toxins) in the blood from a source of infection.
Toxocara canis	A roundworm affecting dogs.
Transplacental	Transfer across the placenta from mother to offspring, e.g. the passage of infection or antibodies.
Trauma	Injury – wounding, shock.
Tumour	A growth or neoplasm.
Umbilical cord	The stalk of blood vessels and tissues that join the developing foetus to the placenta.
Umbilical hernia	The protrusion of an abdominal organ or contents through the umbilicus to lie under the skin outside the abdominal muscles.
Umbilicus	The point on the abdominal wall where the umbilical cord emerged in the developing foetus.
Undershot	Malformation of the jaw where the lower teeth protrude forwards beyond those in the upper jaw – the opposite of 'overshot'.
Uterus	The womb.
Vaccination	The administration of attenuated (weakened) or killed disease organisms to stimulate the production of active antibodies.
Vulva	The external opening of the female genital tract.
Zoonosis	A disease that is communicable from animals to people.